HOME ON THE RANGE

Bryn Parry is one of Britain's best known sporting cartoonists. He has a regular page in *The Shooting Gazette* and his cartoons have appeared in *Horse & Hound*, *Shooting Times* and *The Field*. His work is widely collected by those who appreciate his wry sense of humour and attention to detail.

Also available from Swan Hill Press is Bryn Parry's book of shooting cartoons *Mad Dogs and Englishmen* . . .'an absolutely essential addition to every sportsman's bookshelf – or loo. There can be no-one who so brilliantly and hilariously captures the flavour of the sport and its people'

The Shooting Gazette

HOME ON THE RANGE

CAST IRON RECIPES FOR SUCCESS

EMMA & BRYN PARRY

SWAN·HILL
PRESS

This book is dedicated
to my Mother

Illustrations copyright © 2002 Bryn Parry
Text copyright © 2002 Emma Parry
First published in the UK in 2002 by
Swan Hill Press, an imprint of Quiller Publishing Ltd.

British Library Cataloguing-in-Publication Data
    A catalogue record for this book
    is available from the British Library

ISBN 1 904057 09 8

Printed in Italy

Swan Hill Press
an imprint of Quiller Publishing Ltd.
Wykey House, Wykey, Shrewsbury, SY4 1JA, England
Tel: 01939 261616 Fax: 01939 261606
E-mail: info@quillerbooks.com
Website: www.swanhillbooks.com

Contents

Entrée

I am not a trained cook, and the only lessons I've had took place at school when I was 12. I remember proudly bringing home a bowl of 'Spanish Rice' and was mortified when my mother promptly threw it into the dog bowl. Things have progressed a little since then, you'll be glad to know. I do want to emphasise that this is not a 'serious' cookery book, as I am simply not qualified to write such a thing. Instead I have relied upon the tried and tested recipes of 20 years worth of my own experience, and those of my friends and family. These are definitive, 'cast iron' recipes which work. They are more kitchen suppers than smart dinner parties, and are meant to be as hassle free as possible. They may not be cutting edge, but they are wholesome and delicious.

I married Bryn at 21 and although I had some pretty hit or miss attempts at trying new recipes, I knew I could make good pastry and bake cakes without mishap. My mother also taught me how to cook pasta, which certainly saved the day when we first got married! Experience has given me the confidence to cope with any mistakes – a scattering of raspberries and a light dusting of icing sugar will transform a sunken cake into a delectable pudding.

With a husband, 3 children and a full time job, I also know that I don't have all day to cook something delicious. In an everyday situation, nothing should take more than half an hour. I find cooking therapeutic, and like the act of chopping veg or making bread – it can be very soothing. I also think it's important to show the children how easy it is to prepare a nutritious supper using fresh ingredients, and not to expect everything to go from the freezer to the microwave. They are growing up fast, and our eldest daughter Sophie has had her baptism of culinary fire working as a chalet girl.

How we cook often reflects our upbringing. My mother's motto is 'if you can read, you can cook', and she is right. Her childhood was in India, but she spent her adult life as a diplomat's wife, living in the Middle East, the Far East, Africa, Italy and Outer Mongolia (seriously!). I benefited from all these childhood experiences and have been able to add a few of my own, from living in Australia and making frequent trips to America. The result is a personal repertoire of failsafe recipes that won't let you down – I hope you enjoy them.

Special thanks to Andrew Johnston, whose idea it was, and to Gilly and Victoria, who had the thankless task of editing the book. Last but by no means least to Bryn, for his encouragement, support and illustrations!

The book could not have been written without the help of the following friends – thank you for your invaluable contributions:

Anne Ponsonby, Doreen Batten, Belinda Mitchell, Sophie & Louisa Parry, Gilly Johnston, Jessica Drummond-Smith, Louise Oxley, Julie Riley, Charlotte Miller, Mandy Mitchell, Monique Gudgeon, Brigitte Donaldson and Mark Merison. Special thanks to Sophie, Tom and Louisa for their recipe testing skills, and to Mango and Pickle for their appreciation of the disasters.

Emma Parry

Dogs' Biographies

Pickle

Pickle is an enthusiast. He is a cheerful member of the kitchen staff and prepared to take on tasks that might be considered to be somewhat menial. He is keen on all Game, especially rabbits and very little else. His hobbies include walking, running, digging and rabbits.

Mango

Although trained as a Gun Dog, Mango's greatest passion is food. Most of her days, both awake and asleep, are spent in the kitchen where she displays a remarkable interest in cooking. She is something of a gourmet and relishes a wide variety of menus, especially Game but draws the line at mushrooms. She lists her other interests as picking up, walking, modelling and philosophy.

CHAPTER 1

Breakfast and Brunch

How many times have we been told that breakfast is the most important meal of the day? For most of us, breakfast is at best a bowlful of cereal and maybe some toast. Thank goodness for weekends, when we do have the time to enjoy something a bit more special. There are occasions when nothing but a good fry-up is needed, or you suddenly get the craving for pancakes. I hope these suggestions inspire you to try something different.

SOPHIE'S BREAKFAST ROLLS

My thanks to daughter Sophie for this recipe, who makes these on her rare visits home! They don't take long to make – the dough can even be made the night before and left in the fridge to rise. Then all you have to do in the morning is allow the dough to reach room temperature before knocking down and making into shapes.

Makes 16 rolls

1 lb (450g) strong white flour
2 teaspoons salt
1 sachet easy-blend dried yeast
2 oz (50g) butter
¼ pint (150ml) milk, warm
¼ pint (150ml) water, hand hot
1 egg, beaten

Preheat the oven to 220°C/Gas mark 7/Aga equivalent.

Sift the flour into a mixing bowl, rub in the butter and add the salt and yeast. Give the flour mixture a good stir before adding the liquid. Measure the milk and warm gently in a saucepan. Add the hot water to the milk and then add the liquid a little at a time to the flour (you may not need to use all of it). Use your hands to mix it into a ball, remove from the bowl and start kneading on a lightly floured surface. After about 5-10 minutes return to the mixing bowl (washed first in hot water, dried and lightly oiled). Cover with cling film and leave in a warm place to double in size.

When the dough has risen, knock back with your fist and shape into a ball. Cut in half, then in quarters until you have 16 'slices' (like an orange segment). Take a slice and make into any or all of the following shapes:
S shape – roll into a long sausage shape and bend into an S
Plait – divide one slice into three and plait together
Twist – divide one slice into two and twist together
Christmas shapes – roll the dough until it's about ½ inch thick and make shapes using assorted Christmas cutters, e.g. reindeer, angels etc.

When you've made your required shapes, place on a baking tray and cover with cling film. Leave to puff up, then brush with beaten egg and place in a hot oven for about 10 minutes, or until golden. Serve warm from the oven.

CONTINENTAL BREAKFAST

One of the things I enjoy about going to Europe, whether it's business or pleasure, is knowing that breakfast will be different. The daily visits to the boulangerie were looked upon with great excitement when the children were little, so recreate a little of that relaxed approach to life – make a frothy cappuccino and indulge in a delicious pain-au-raisin. Shut your eyes, and you could almost be in Paris!

When you have a full house for the weekend and you know people will appear at different times of the morning, lay out a typical continental breakfast, and watch how fast it disappears.

Fresh fruit salad – use whatever fruits are available (e.g. grapes, melon, pineapple, banana, strawberries)
Selection of plain and fruit yoghurts
Croissants, pain-au-chocolat, Danish pastries.
Bagels – delicious lightly toasted with cream cheese and smoked salmon
Slivers of cheese and thin ham on a platter
Selection of conserves and honey

EGGY BREAD

This is properly known as French Toast, but we've always called it Eggy Bread.

Serves 4

4 slices white bread, cut into triangles
4 eggs, beaten
Salt and pepper
1 tablespoon sunflower oil

Whisk the eggs into a large bowl and season with salt and pepper. Dip the bread into the egg mixture until thoroughly covered. Heat a large frying pan with a drop of sunflower oil and when hot, fry the eggy bread slices until golden brown. Serve immediately (N.B. tomato ketchup is an obligatory extra!).

BACON BUTTIES

Essential late night party food at 4 a.m.!

Serves 2

4 slices of fresh white bread (or one ciabatta bread if you want to be more up-market)
8 slices of quality back bacon
Ketchup (optional)

Grill or fry the rashers. When the bacon is crispy round the edges, slap onto one slice of buttered bread or toast (if you like, spread with ketchup first). Top with the remaining slice and go straight to heaven.

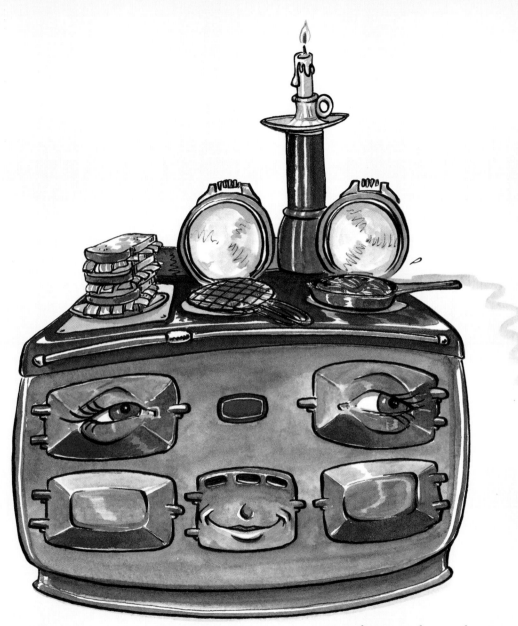

Knocking up bacon butties

AMERICAN PANCAKES WITH MAPLE SYRUP

You need to really indulge yourself and have about 4 pancakes piled up with sliced bananas, sliced strawberries (in season) and a generous amount of maple syrup drooling over them. To be really authentic you could also serve them with some crispy, streaky bacon.

Serves 4 (makes about 16 pancakes)

8 oz (225g) self-raising flour
2 large eggs, beaten
2 teaspoons sugar
Just over ½ pint milk (300ml)
Knob of butter or oil for frying
A bottle of maple syrup

The easiest method is to place the flour, eggs, sugar and milk in a food processor and whizz for a few seconds until well blended and the consistency of thick cream. Transfer the mixture to a jug.

Heat a small, heavy frying pan with a drop of oil or butter. When hot, place a spoonful of the batter in the pan and cook for about 2-3 minutes – when it starts to bubble it's time to turn over; cook for a further minute or two or until the pancake is golden brown. Pile them up on a hot plate and eat immediately!

SMOOTHIES

Every now and then (particularly after an indulgent weekend) I crave something incredibly healthy. Smoothies are just that – pure health in a glass! Some are ideal for breakfast; others can be enjoyed as a healthy snack at any time of the day. They are great for teenagers (or anyone else, come to that) who need a quick energy fix. Do experiment and try other combinations – I think most fruits work well together.

1 banana	**or**	1 banana
2 oz (50g) strawberries		Handful of frozen
2 oz (50g) pineapple chunks		tropical fruits
4 ice cubes		¼ pint (150ml) orange juice

Whizz in a blender until smooth

BANANA SMOOTHIE

1 banana
4 fl oz (120ml) plain yoghurt
1 teaspoon pure vanilla extract
4 ice cubes

RASPBERRY SMOOTHIE

4 oz (110g) raspberries
4 fl oz (120ml) raspberry yoghurt
1 banana
4 ice cubes

Blend all the ingredients together until smooth and creamy.

KEDGEREE

This is the perfect brunch dish, but if you wanted to cook it for supper you could add some prawns and frozen peas.

Serves 4

1 lb (450g) undyed smoked haddock
¼ pint (150ml) water
8 oz (225g) Basmati rice
2 oz (50g) butter
1 onion, chopped
1 tablespoon curry powder
4 hard boiled eggs
Small bunch of chopped parsley
Tablespoon chopped chives
1 lemon
Salt and pepper

Place the haddock in a baking tray. Add the water and place in a medium hot oven so that it gently poaches for about 10 minutes or until the fish is just beginning to cook through. Alternatively you could place the fish in a frying pan and heat gently until it flakes. Drain, place the fish on a plate and remove any bones or skin. Roughly flake with a fork and put aside. Put the eggs on to boil in a small pan and cook until hard (about 10 minutes), and at the same time cook the rice in a saucepan of boiling, salted water for about 10-12 minutes. If you want to add colour, you could add a pinch of turmeric to the boiling water, which will turn the rice yellow.
When cooked, rinse and drain the rice in a sieve. Melt the butter in a large frying pan and add the chopped onion. Soften the onion and then add the curry powder. Stir in the flaked fish, cooked rice, parsley and seasoning. Heat through for a few minutes and then pile the kedgeree onto a warmed platter. Decorate with quartered hard-boiled eggs, chopped parsley, some lemon wedges and a few chopped chives over the top.

CARROT CAKE MUFFINS

I got hooked on muffins when we started visiting New York on a regular basis. On our way to the Convention Center we would do what New Yorkers do – buy huge muffins and eat them on the way to work. These aren't quite as big as the American version but are just as mouthwatering. It is worth using paper muffin liners, as they will save you a lot of time and effort when it comes to washing up.

The basic principles of muffin making are to weigh out the dry ingredients in one bowl, the liquid ingredients in another and then combine them together. Don't worry if they look a bit lumpy and don't over-beat the mixture – just stir a couple of times to mix everything together.

Makes about 8 large muffins or 12 mini muffins

6 oz (175g) plain flour
2 oz (50g) wholemeal flour
2 teaspoons baking powder
Zest of 1 orange
4 oz (110g) grated carrot
4 oz (110g) sultanas

4oz (110g) soft brown sugar
1 large egg, beaten
2 tablespoons vegetable oil
½ pint (275ml) milk
Pinch of salt

Preheat the oven to 200°C/Gas mark 6/Aga equivalent.

Sift both flours and the baking powder into a mixing bowl. Add the sugar, grated carrots, sultanas, orange zest and a pinch of salt. In another bowl, gently whisk together the milk, oil and beaten egg. Pour the milky mixture into the dry ingredients and stir it a couple of times. It will look lumpy at this stage but don't worry. Spoon into muffin paper cases and cook for about 15-20 minutes. Cool for 5 minutes, then place on a wire rack. These taste even better the next day.

BLUEBERRY MUFFINS

As I can never seem to find buttermilk, I use a mix of milk and yoghurt to achieve the same effect. Obviously use buttermilk if you can.

Preheat the oven to 200°C/Gas mark 6/Aga equivalent.

8 oz (225g) plain flour
2 teaspoons baking powder
4 oz (110g) soft brown sugar
Pinch salt
4 tablespoons vegetable oil
7 fl oz (200ml) milk and plain
   yoghurt combined
1 egg, beaten
7 oz (200g) fresh blueberries

Sift the dry ingredients in a bowl. Pour in the liquid ingredients and stir lightly. Fold in the blueberries and stir again. Spoon into muffin paper cases and bake for about 15-20 minutes.

Makes approximately 8 large muffins.

EGG AND CHIP BANJO

Perfect for late night parties or when returning back to base after a patrol (courtesy of Bryn's Northern Ireland war stories!). N.B. Not for the faint-hearted!

Serves 1

Handful of piping hot oven ready chips
2 eggs, fried
2 slices thickly buttered white bread
Ketchup or Brown sauce (optional!)

Fry the eggs and slap onto one piece of bread. Top with chips and sauce. Add remaining slice of bread, squash flat so that the eggs burst and soak into the chips and bread. Don't even think of the calories.

PORRIDGE

When the weather is really cold and frosty, nothing beats a hot bowl of porridge. I like it with a little extra milk and demerara sugar; the children pour on golden syrup and as for Bryn…he does enjoy the occasional shot of whisky with his porridge (and perhaps a dollop of cream for extra indulgence).

SAUSAGE SARNIE

Serves 2

1 ciabatta bread
4 pork sausages
Dijon mustard
Roasted red peppers

Grill the sausages until brown and crisp. Toast the ciabatta bread, cut in half and spread with Dijon mustard. Cut the sausages in half and lay over the mustard. Top with roasted red peppers and place the other ciabatta half on top.

SMOKED HADDOCK AND POACHED EGG

Serves 1

1 smoked haddock fillet, approx 6 oz (175g)
1 egg, poached
2 slices of brown bread and butter

Place the haddock in a pan with just enough water to half cover it. Poach for about 5 minutes, remove from the pan and keep warm. Poach the egg in the same water as the haddock, and when ready, place on top of the haddock. Serve with brown bread and butter.

KIPPERS AND BUTTERED BROWN BREAD

Serves 1

If you have an Aga, thank your lucky stars, as you won't have a house smelling of kipper!

1 smoked kipper (undyed)
2 slices of brown bread and butter
1 pot of tea (to be really traditional)

Place the kipper in a baking tray and add a knob of butter on top. Bake in moderate oven for 10-15 minutes or grill (if you can stand it) for about 5 minutes each side. Serve with slices of brown bread and butter, washed down with a strong cup of tea.

SCRAMBLED EGG AND SMOKED SALMON

Equally delicious as a Sunday night snack.

Serves 2

4 eggs, beaten
2 slices smoked salmon, cut into small pieces
Salt and pepper
Butter

Melt a knob of butter in a pan and add the eggs. Stir for about 2 minutes, until scrambled. Add the smoked salmon and season with salt and freshly ground black pepper. Serve on a slice of toast and eat immediately.

RIFLE BRIGADE SAVOURY

Bryn thought you might all benefit from a little Regimental History….

After the Battle of Waterloo the officers fancied a spot of breakfast, but only had bread, butter, cheese and Guinness in their rations. So they toasted the bread, spread it with butter and grated some cheese over the top. It was then grilled until the cheese was bubbling, and presumably at this stage some young whippersnapper of a subaltern decided to pour some hot Guinness over the top. Bryn assures me that it tastes superb, but I have to admit I have never tried it!

The ironing was done as if by magic

CHAPTER 2

Soups and Starters

I don't know about you, but sometimes the thought of doing a starter throws me into a panic and my mind goes blank. Here are some reliable and very easy starters to help with the inspiration.

GAZPACHO

This classic Andalusian soup is bursting with flavour. Make it well ahead of time as it needs to be well chilled before serving.

Serves 6

400g tin chopped tomatoes
1 small, day old white loaf, crusts removed
1 red pepper, de-seeded and chopped
1 cucumber
2-3 cloves garlic, peeled and chopped
18 fl oz (510ml) fresh tomato juice
2 fl oz (55ml) olive oil
1 tablespoon red wine vinegar
18 fl oz (510ml) water
Salt and pepper
Basil leaves

For the garnishes
1 green pepper, de-seeded and chopped
3 skinned, de-seeded tomatoes, diced
1 red onion, peeled and finely chopped
2 oz (50g) black olives, stoned and chopped
Olive oil, for croutons made with left over bread
Basil leaves

Cut the loaf of bread in half. Put one half in a food processor and blitz to form breadcrumbs; cut the remaining half into cubes for making croutons later.

Tip the breadcrumbs into a large mixing bowl. Chop the pepper and dice half a cucumber (the other half you keep until later). Put the garlic, pepper, a handful of basil and the chopped cucumber into the processor and whizz to a pulp; add the tinned tomatoes and blend until the mixture is smooth. Pour this over the breadcrumbs and add the tomato juice and water. Mix well and stir in the vinegar, olive oil and seasoning. Chill thoroughly.

To make the garnishes: Dice the olives, the remaining cucumber and green pepper and place in separate bowls. Place the diced bread on a baking tray, drizzle with olive oil and bake in a hot oven for about 10 minutes, or until the croutons are golden brown. Drain on kitchen paper until cold.

To serve, pour the soup into individual bowls and scatter over a little torn basil. Place the bowls of garnishes on the table and allow people to help themselves.

PARSNIP SOUP

The combination of curry paste (or powder) and parsnips makes this a very popular winter soup.

Serves 6

3 tablespoons olive oil
1 tablespoon curry paste, or 1½ teaspoons curry powder
1 medium onion, peeled and chopped
1½ lb (750g) medium sized parsnips, peeled, trimmed
    and sliced
430g tin consommé soup, diluted with 1 can water
    – or the equivalent in chicken stock
Salt and freshly ground black pepper
5 fl oz (142ml carton) single cream
Handful of chopped parsley

In a large heavy pan, fry the onion in the olive oil and add the curry powder or paste. Add the parsnips, place the lid on and sweat until the vegetables are tender. Pour in the consommé and water, or chicken stock, and simmer until the vegetables are cooked. Season to taste. Cool a little before placing in a blender or food processor. Return to the pan and gently stir in the cream. Sprinkle over a little chopped parsley. This soup can either be served hot or chilled.

FRENCH ONION SOUP

This is a really heart-warming soup on a cold winter's day.

Serves 6

4 large Spanish onions, peeled and sliced
2 oz (50g) butter
2 tablespoons olive oil
1 teaspoon demerara sugar
2 x 295g tins condensed consommé mixed with 1 pint
    (570ml) water
½ pint (275ml) white wine
Salt and pepper
1 French bread stick, cut in diagonal slices
2 cloves garlic, crushed
6 oz (175g) Gruyère cheese

Heat the butter and olive oil in a heavy casserole pan and add the sliced onions. Add the sugar and cook on a high heat for about 5 minutes. Reduce the heat and simmer gently for about 30 minutes. Mix the consommé with the water and add to the onions. Add the white wine, salt and pepper and simmer gently for about 1 hour. Just before serving, toast the slices of bread and rub over with garlic. Grate the Gruyère over the slices and grill until brown and bubbling. Pour the soup into warm bowls and top each bowl with a slice of cheesy toast.

TURKEY KNUCKLE SOUP

This soup is inspired by my mother-in-law's legendary post-Christmas soup, which more often than not might well contain the odd knuckle! It is a brilliant way to use up all the leftovers, and means you don't have to think about lunch the next day. Make good use of the turkey carcass by making up some stock before you begin.

Place all the left-overs in your largest saucepan (and by that I mean literally all the bits from the Christmas dinner – roast potatoes, parsnips, the dark meat from the turkey, gravy, bread sauce, the dreaded brussels sprouts, carrots, cranberry sauce – have I left out anything?). Cover with turkey stock. Bring to the boil and then simmer gently until it has become nice and soupified. Add seasoning to taste and blast in the blender until it's how you like it – totally smooth or slightly chunky. Serve with plenty of crusty French bread and heave a sigh of relief that there is now more space in your fridge.

BROCCOLI SOUP

Quick and easy – the best kind of soup to make!

Serves 4 as a starter, or 2 as a main soup for lunch

1 oz (25g) butter
1 large head of broccoli (broken into florets, stalks removed)
2 medium potatoes, peeled and diced
1 medium onion, peeled and finely chopped
1½ pints (845ml) vegetable stock (I use the invaluable Swiss Marigold stock)
2–3 tablespoons crème fraîche

Heat the butter in a pan and add the onions and potatoes. Fry for a few minutes and add the broccoli. Put the pan lid on and sweat the vegetables for about 5 minutes. Add the stock and bring to the boil. Simmer until the vegetables are soft; season with salt and pepper.
Place in a food processor and whizz for a few seconds. Serve in warm bowls with a dollop of crème fraîche on top.

DELICIOUS THAI SOUP

Serves 4

2 chicken breasts, skinned
2 pints (1.2 litres) chicken stock
400ml tin of coconut milk
5 tablespoons of lemon or lime juice
2 red chillies
3 garlic cloves, peeled and crushed
1 packet fresh bean sprouts
150g pack 'straight to wok' thread noodles – or cook medium egg
    noodles, rinse and have ready to use
4 oz (110g) prawns
2 inch (5cm) piece fresh ginger, peeled and finely grated
1 packet of baby spinach leaves (ready washed)
Handful of coriander leaves, chopped
Salt and pepper
2 tablespoons sunflower oil

Heat the stock in a pan; add the coconut milk and half the lemon or lime
juice. Prepare the chillies by cutting them in half and discarding the seeds,
and then chop very finely. Have the grated ginger and crushed garlic ready.
Slice the chicken breasts very thinly. Place a handful of spinach leaves
in each bowl.

Heat the oil in a wok and add the grated ginger and crushed garlic. Add the
chicken slices and stir-fry for about 2 minutes. Add the chillies and bean
sprouts and cook for a further 2 minutes. Add the coconut stock liquid,
prawns and noodles. Bring to the boil, remove from the heat, season with
salt and pepper and add more lemon or lime juice to taste. Ladle onto the
spinach leaves and sprinkle generously with chopped coriander.

PRAWN PATE

I use frozen prawns for this pâté – they
taste better if you defrost them in the
fridge overnight.

Serves 4

8 oz (225g) prawns
4 oz (110g) butter, softened
2 tablespoons mayonnaise
3 tablespoons cream cheese
Salt and pepper
Pinch of paprika
1 teaspoon chopped chives
Lemon and parsley to garnish

I use a food processor to make this.
Process the butter, mayonnaise and
cream cheese until smooth. Add the
prawns, but only pulse for a second or
two – you don't want mushy prawns!
Season with salt and pepper, a pinch
of paprika and teaspoon of chopped
chives. Place the mixture in small
ramekins and chill in the fridge for about
an hour before serving. Garnish with a
twist of lemon and a sprig of parsley.

The homework helper

MUSHROOM RAVIOLI ON A BED OF WILTED BABY SPINACH

I love what's on offer at any major supermarket - the range of ravioli is breathtaking and has solved many a problem for me. Dead easy and looks amazing.

Serves 4-6

Knob of butter
2 x 250g packets of fresh mushroom ravioli
200g crème fraîche
4-6 large flat mushrooms - whatever is available - with their stalks removed
1 packet of baby spinach leaves (ready washed)
Approx 2 oz (50g) Parmesan shavings
Salt and pepper

Bake the mushrooms in the oven with a knob of butter on each one (if you like garlic, add a sprinkling of chopped garlic over the butter). Cook for about 10 minutes. Remove, but don't wash up the baking tray - you will need it later.

Cook the ravioli according to the packet - it usually only takes a few minutes. Drain and keep warm in the pan.

Put the spinach in a colander and very quickly wilt over a pan of boiling water. You have to be quick here! Remove and lay out a small heap of wilted spinach on each plate. Then add the mushroom with the ravioli sitting in the mushroom 'dip'.

Pour the tub of crème fraîche into the baking tray that you cooked the mushrooms in and heat through quickly. Season to taste and pour a little over each pile of ravioli. Scatter a few Parmesan shavings over each mushroom.

SMOKED SALMON RAVIOLI

Another quick cheat here, but no apologies needed. Quality supermarkets sell a good variety of ravioli so it's worth shopping around.

Serves 3-4

250g pack of fresh smoked salmon ravioli
100g crème fraîche
150g packet of smoked salmon trimmings
Small bag of watercress

Cook the ravioli according to the packet. Drain and leave in saucepan. Add the crème fraîche to the ravioli and gently cook for a few minutes. Pile the ravioli on each plate and scatter the smoked salmon trimmings artistically on top. Add a few stalks of watercress to add contrast to the colour. Serve with some warm ciabatta.

SAVOURY PROFITEROLES

2½ oz (60g) plain flour
2 oz (50g) butter, cut into pieces
2 eggs, well beaten
¼ pint (150ml) cold water

Makes approximately 18, so would serve 6 as a starter

Preheat the oven to 200°C/Gas mark 6/Aga equivalent.

Sieve the flour onto a piece of greaseproof paper (folded) so that you can 'shoot' the flour into the pan later.

Put the water in a saucepan, add the butter and melt over a moderate heat. As soon as the mixture has melted and come to the boil, turn off the heat and 'shoot' the flour all at once into the pan. With a wooden spoon, beat the mixture vigorously. Continue beating until the paste leaves the side of the pan (this takes less than a minute). Cool slightly and then beat in the eggs a little at a time.

Place teaspoons of choux pastry onto baking trays, lined with parchment paper (non-stick) and bake for about 15 minutes, or until puffed up, crisp and golden in colour. Make a slit in the side to let the steam out and allow to cool on a wire rack. Stuff each profiterole with any of the following:

Mix half a tub of cream cheese with 2-3 tablespoons of crème fraîche and mix in a handful of chopped chives. Place 3 profiteroles on each plate and serve with the QUICK TOMATO SAUCE and decorate with basil leaves.

Alternatively try stuffing with egg mayonnaise, prawns or coronation chicken.

QUICK TOMATO SAUCE

2 tablespoons olive oil
3 garlic cloves, peeled and finely
  chopped
400g tin of tomatoes, ready
  chopped
2-3 basil leaves
1 tablespoon tomato pureé
Salt and freshly ground
  black pepper

Heat the olive oil in a heavy pan and sauté the garlic for about a minute. Add the tomatoes and cook on a high heat for 10 minutes. Add the rest of the ingredients and simmer for a further few minutes. If you like a smoother sauce, either whizz in a food processor or strain through a sieve. Serve either hot or cold. Season with salt and freshly ground black pepper.

SMOKED HADDOCK POTS WITH LEMON DRESSED LEAVES

Serves 6

8 oz (225g) undyed smoked haddock
1 bay leaf
Salt and pepper
½ pint (275ml) milk
5 fl oz (142ml carton) double cream
3 large egg yolks
1 tablespoon chopped chives
Pinch of nutmeg
1 bag of ready washed salad leaves

For the dressing:
1 tablespoon lemon juice
1 tablespoon olive oil
1 level tablespoon wholegrain mustard
Salt and pepper

Preheat the oven to 170°C/Gas mark 3/Aga equivalent.

Lightly butter 6 ramekin dishes. Place the haddock in a pan. Pour over the milk, add the bay leaf and poach for 5 minutes. Remove the fish and using a fork, flake the fish onto a plate, removing any skin and fish-bones. Reserve the milk, as you will need this later. Place the fish in equal amounts into the ramekins and set aside.

Place the cream in a mixing bowl and add the egg yolks, chives, nutmeg. Whisk everything together and add the reserved milk (remove the bay leaf). Pour this mixture over the fish placed in the ramekins. Using a fork, gently lift the bits of fish so that they are not sitting at the bottom of the ramekin. Place the ramekins on a baking sheet and bake for 15-20 minutes or until set in the centre and golden brown on the outside.

Rest for 10 minutes before serving. Then turn them out onto serving plates. Arrange some salad leaves around the haddock creams. Mix all the dressing ingredients in a jar and shake. Pour over the salad just before serving.

SMOKED MACKEREL PATE

Pâtés seem to have gone out of fashion, but they are quick to make and served with plenty of toast, go down a treat.

Serves 6

10 oz (275g) smoked mackerel fillets
2 oz (50g) unsalted softened butter
3 tablespoons creamed horseradish
2 tablespoons single cream
Pepper

Flake the mackerel into a bowl, removing any skin or small bones. Add the rest of the ingredients and either blend in a food processor or mash with a fork until well mixed. Season with freshly ground black pepper and spoon into small ramekins. Cover with cling film and chill in the fridge until required.

SARDINE AND LEMON PATE

Cheap and cheerful!

Serves 4

3 oz (75g) butter, softened
3 oz (75g) cream cheese
7 oz (200g) sardines (or 2 tins worth)
2 tablespoons creamed horseradish sauce
Juice of 1 lemon
Salt and pepper
Chives, for garnishing

Cream the butter and cream cheese together, then drain the sardines and mash them roughly with a fork. Add to the butter and cream cheese mixture and mix in the horseradish. Next stir in 3 tablespoons of lemon juice and a grind or two of black pepper and a little salt. Add a little more lemon juice to taste. Garnish with some snipped chives. Serve with plenty of granary toast and butter.

PROSCUITTO E MELONE

This has to be the easiest starter around. It was a particular favourite of my late father.

1 large, ripe melon
Proscuitto, allow 2-3 slices per person

Cut the melon into slices and skim off the seeds. Arrange the slices of Proscuitto beside it, and there you have it!

ANTIPASTI

When all else fails and you just aren't inspired, try this as a starter. The Italians know a thing or two about how to start off a meal, and here are a few suggestions – the main thing is that everyone feels free to help themselves and enjoy the selections on offer.

A selection of green and black olives
Proscuitto
Salami
Mozzarella
Sun-dried tomatoes
Roasted red and yellow peppers, cut into
    slices
Roasted cherry tomatoes
Tiger prawns, in their shells (grilled and
    smothered in hot garlicky butter)
Plenty of warm, fresh bread.

The only work involved is to roast the peppers and cherry tomatoes and grill the prawns. If you were in a bread-making mood, how about some home made focaccia or olive bread. Or just go out and buy a good selection of freshly made bread.

Arrange a selection of this type of food on a large platter. Place in the centre of the table, pour out the wine, sit back and relax!

BRUSCHETTA

This is one of my favourite ways of doing a starter and one that brings back fond memories of Italy.

Use either a good rustic French bread stick or ciabatta bread. Cut fairly thick slices on the diagonal and rub with garlic. Heat a griddle pan with a little olive oil and quickly toast the bread on both sides - ideally showing the brown griddle marks. Top with any of the following:

Serves 4-6

Toppings

8 tomatoes, skins and seeds removed and roughly chopped
5 oz (150g) ball of mozzarella, drained and roughly chopped
Fresh basil leaves

Vinaigrette
Freshly ground salt and pepper
6 black olives
1 oz (25g) Parmesan shavings

Mix the tomatoes and mozzarella in a bowl and add a little homemade vinaigrette and marinade for a few minutes. Season well and then spoon onto the bread. You could also add some chopped black olives to the mixture. Top with a basil leaf.

Variations:

Place strips of mozzarella over the tomatoes and grill until just beginning to melt.

Spread a little roasted red pepper paste over the bread, add some Proscuitto and strips of roasted peppers (either roast some red and yellow peppers in some olive oil or buy a jar of good quality Italian roasted peppers). Add a few shavings of Parmesan and bake in a hot oven for about 5 minutes.

WARM GOAT'S CHEESE SALAD

Serves 4-6

Approx 9 oz (250g) goat's cheese log (including the rind), cut into 4-6 slices
1 bunch of watercress
Bag of rocket leaves
1 small packet of chopped walnuts
Parmesan shavings

Wholegrain Mustard Dressing

4 tablespoons olive oil
1 tablespoon white wine vinegar
1 teaspoon wholegrain mustard
1 teaspoon sugar
Salt and freshly ground pepper to taste

Place the slices of goat's cheese on a baking tray and grill until just going brown. Arrange a mixture of the leaves on each individual plate and top with the goat's cheese. Drizzle the wholegrain mustard dressing over the salad and scatter the chopped walnuts on top. Sprinkle with Parmesan shavings and serve with some crusty bread.

The builders were in

TOMATO RING MOULD FILLED WITH PRAWNS

This is my mother's recipe and one that I used for every dinner party when we first got married (because I <u>knew</u> it worked).

Serves 6–8

1 pint (570ml) good quality fresh tomato juice
1 tablespoon Worcestershire sauce
Dash of Tabasco sauce
Salt and freshly ground pepper
1 sachet of gelatine
8 oz (225g) of prawns – prawns can be frozen, but use the
    tiger prawns as they have more substance to them
    (thaw thoroughly and drain well before using)
1 tin of crabmeat, drained
Lemon wedges
Additional fresh prawns for decoration (approx 12)
1 bag of rocket leaves for decoration

Measure the tomato juice in a jug and add the Tabasco and Worcestershire sauce and seasoning. In a cup, dissolve the gelatine in some hot water until it goes transparent. Add to the tomato mixture, mix well and pour into the ring mould. Cover with cling film and leave to set in the fridge for several hours. While that is setting, make the mayo mixture for the seafood.

Mayo mixture:
4 tablespoons mayonnaise
4 tablespoons single cream
1-2 teaspoons tomato purée
1 tablespoon tomato ketchup
Juice of 1 fresh lemon
Dash of Worcestershire sauce
Salt and pepper.

Mix all these ingredients together and season to taste. Add the defrosted and drained prawns and the crabmeat and mix thoroughly.

Have a large round platter ready. Remove the ring mould from the fridge and quickly dip the bottom of the mould in a washing up bowl of hot water so that it slides out easily. Invert the platter onto the ring mould and flip over – with luck, it will remain intact! Fill the middle with the seafood mixture and scatter some rocket around the side. Decorate the top of the tomato ring with fresh prawns and lemon wedges. Serve with brown bread and butter.

SMOKED HADDOCK AND EGG MOUSSE

I make this in a ring mould – it's perfect either as a starter or a light lunch.

Serves 4

Bay leaf
1 lb (450g) undyed smoked haddock
10 fl oz (284ml carton) whipping cream
1 x 295g tin condensed consommé
1 sachet gelatine
3 hard boiled eggs
5 fl oz (150ml) mayonnaise

Freshly ground pepper
Few drops of Tabasco
1 tablespoon chopped parsley
Lemon wedges and extra parsley for
    decoration
1 bag of rocket leaves or watercress
Vinaigrette

Cover the haddock with water and a bay leaf and poach until the fish is flaky. Remove skin and fish bones and flake with a fork. Allow to cool.

Soften the gelatine in a little consommé over a warm heat until it has dissolved. Add the gelatine mixture to the rest of the consommé.

Roughly chop the eggs. Combine two thirds of the consommé with the cooked haddock, eggs and parsley. The remaining consommé can be poured into the bottom of the ring mould and allowed to set in the fridge.

Season the fish and egg mixture with pepper and Tabasco and place in a food processor. Pulse until everything is coarsely chopped but not over-processed. Turn into a bowl and refrigerate until the mixture is just beginning to set. Whisk the cream until thick. Fold the mayonnaise and cream into the just-setting mousse and turn into the ring mould. Chill until required.

When ready to serve, turn onto a platter and fill the middle with watercress or rocket leaves tossed in a light vinaigrette. Decorate the top with lemon wedges and chopped parsley.

WATERCRESS MOUSSE

This is perfect to make ahead of time. It's very quick to make and can then sit in the fridge until you're ready to serve.

Serves 4

8 oz (225g) cream cheese
5 fl oz (150ml) mayonnaise
2 bunches of watercress, washed
1 sachet of gelatine dissolved in
    ½ pint (275ml) of chicken stock
10 fl oz (284ml carton) whipping
    cream
Dash of Worcestershire sauce
Salt and pepper

Place the cream cheese and watercress in a food processor and blend until smooth. Add the gelatine stock and process for a few seconds. Lightly whip the cream in a bowl and fold into the watercress mixture. Season with salt and pepper and a dash of Worcestershire sauce, and place in a ring mould or ramekins. Chill for several hours. Just before serving, turn out onto a platter (if using a ring mould) and decorate with a few watercress leaves.

SMOKED SALMON CARPACCIO

This is simplicity itself and tastes wonderful.

Serves 6

1½ lb (700g) smoked salmon (or smoked trout)
4 tablespoons light olive oil
3-4 tablespoons freshly squeezed lemon juice
1 lemon, cut into wedges
4 tablespoons chopped chives
Freshly ground black pepper

Loosely arrange the smoked salmon in a single layer on a large platter. Drizzle with olive oil and sprinkle with chives and plenty of black pepper. This can be done a couple of hours in advance. 30 minutes before serving, drizzle with lemon juice and decorate with lemon wedges. Serve with plenty of brown bread and butter.

CELERIAC SALAD WITH PROSCUITTO

Serves 4

1 large celeriac
2-3 round tablespoons mayonnaise
1 teaspoon Dijon mustard
12 slices Proscuitto

Peel the celeriac, cut into narrow slices and then into batons. Add to a pan of boiling, salted water and blanch for 2-3 minutes. Drain in a colander and allow to cool. Blend together the mayonnaise and mustard and toss the celeriac into the dressing.

Arrange 3 slices of Proscuitto on individual plates and place a large spoonful of the salad beside it.

CHAPTER 3

Sensational Salads

When the weather finally warms up, enjoy the colours and flavours of these salads. Some can be used as an accompaniment to grilled meat or fish; others can just be enjoyed as a meal in themselves.

TOMATO, AVOCADO AND MOZZARELLA SALAD

We eat this nearly every day in the summer – it just can't be beaten.

Serves 4-6

4-6 large tomatoes – preferably home grown, but if not then buy the ones with the most flavour. Make sure they are at room temperature and not straight from the fridge – the flavours will come out more if they aren't too cold.

2 x 150g packets mozzarella, drained and sliced
2 small ripe avocados
Basil leaves
Salt and freshly ground black pepper

Dressing
5 tablespoons good olive oil
1 tablespoon white wine vinegar
1 teaspoon sugar
1 teaspoon mustard powder
Salt and pepper

Slice the tomatoes and arrange artistically with the sliced mozzarella and avocados on a shallow platter. Season with salt and pepper. Spoon over the dressing and scatter some torn basil leaves over the top. Serve immediately with plenty of crusty bread and some nicely chilled Orvieto Classico!

MIXED BEAN SALAD

I love the colours in this salad – you've got the emerald green beans, the bright yellow sweetcorn and the glossy dark red kidney beans – good enough to paint, let alone eat!

Serves 4

420g tin sweetcorn, drained
420g tin kidney beans, rinsed and drained
8oz (225g) French beans
1 red onion, finely chopped
Handful of freshly chopped parsley
Quantity of wholegrain mustard dressing (see page 28)

Cook the French beans in a pan of salted, boiling water for about 3-4 minutes – they must not be overcooked. Drain in a colander and plunge into another bowl of cold water to prevent them from cooking any further. Leave in the water until you're ready to assemble the salad. Arrange the kidney beans and sweetcorn in a glass bowl, add the cooled and drained French beans and chopped red onion and toss around to mix them all up. Add the chopped parsley, and just before serving pour over the mustard vinaigrette. Mix thoroughly and serve alongside the main dish.

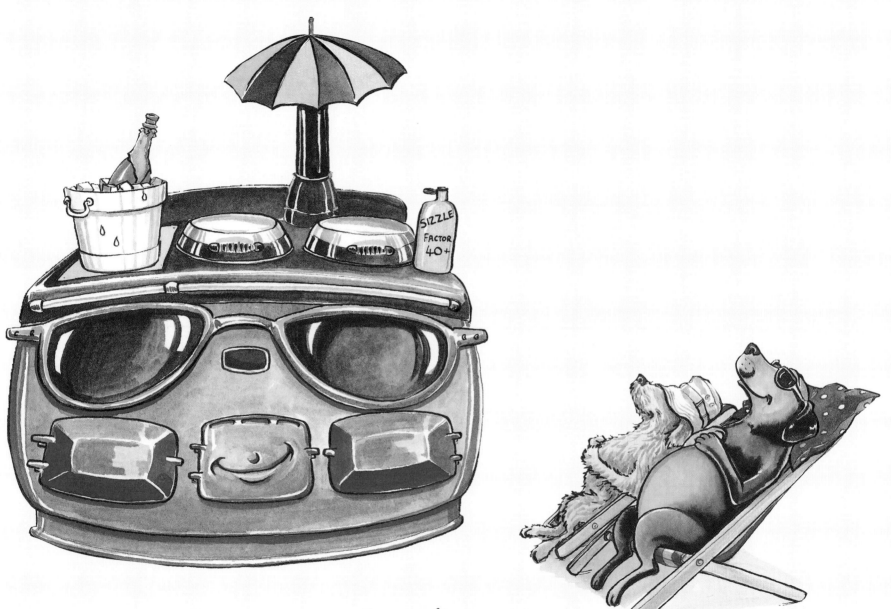

Pretty cool in August

TABBOULEH

Tabbouleh is one of my favourite summer salads. The aroma of freshly chopped mint is glorious and it tastes wonderful too.

Serves 6

8 oz (225) bulgur wheat (also called cracked wheat and is widely available)
4 oz (110g) finely chopped parsley
8 spring onions, finely chopped
½ cucumber, diced
1 lb (450g) tomatoes, skins and seeds removed
2 oz (50g) fresh mint, chopped
Salt and pepper

Dressing:
Juice of 1 lemon
1 crushed clove garlic
6 tablespoons olive oil
1 teaspoon sugar

Put the bulgur wheat in a bowl and cover with cold water. Leave to soak for about 20 minutes or until the grains have swollen. In a small bowl, whisk together the dressing ingredients and set aside. Chop up the spring onions, cucumber and tomatoes. Drain the bulgur wheat in a colander lined with a clean tea towel. Really squeeze the excess water from the wheat until it is as dry as possible.
Place in a shallow platter and add the cucumber, tomatoes, spring onions and chopped mint and parsley. Add the dressing and season with salt and pepper to taste. Toss thoroughly.

SUMMER PEA SALAD

Don't be put off by the long list of ingredients – it really is quite delicious and worth the effort if you want to serve something original.

Serves 6–8

4 oz (110g) black olives, stoned and chopped
1 large red pepper, de-seeded and finely chopped
2 inch (approx 5 cm) fresh ginger, peeled and finely chopped
3 cloves garlic, peeled and finely chopped
1½ lb (700g pack) frozen peas (petit pois)
4 oz (110g) pot candied peel
Juice of one large lemon
Just over ¼ pint (150ml) extra virgin olive oil
Pinch paprika
Large bunch fresh mint, chopped
1 bunch flat leaf parsley, chopped
Salt and pepper

Place everything except the mint and parsley into a large heavy saucepan and cook over a low heat for about 15 minutes, stirring occasionally. Remove from heat and allow to cool. Season and add the chopped mint and parsley. This is best eaten at room temperature.

SUMMER SALAD WITH THAI BEEF

Perfect for informal summer lunches. The oriental Thai dressing really transforms the beef into something quite exotic.

Serves 6

Approx 2 lb (1 kg) fillet of beef, trimmed
Salt and freshly ground black pepper
Olive oil

Thai dressing for the beef:
Handful of mint leaves
Handful of chopped coriander leaves
2 cloves garlic, peeled and finely chopped
2 tablespoons soya sauce
2 tablespoons nam pla (Thai fish sauce)
2 tablespoons lime juice
1½ tablespoons brown sugar
2 red chillies, de-seeded and finely
   chopped

Salad:
1 bag mixed green salad leaves,
   washed and dried
Large bunch asparagus spears, blanched
1 punnet red cherry tomatoes, halved
1 red pepper and 1 yellow pepper,
   roasted and cut into strips
2 dozen quail eggs, hardboiled
Balsamic vinegar
Olive oil
Salt and freshly ground black pepper

Preheat the oven to 220°C/Gas mark 7/Aga equivalent.

Rub the beef with a little olive oil and season well with salt and freshly ground black pepper. Bake in a hot oven for about 25-30 minutes for medium/rare beef. Remove from the oven and set aside to cool. When cool, slice into fine strips.

Place all the ingredients for the dressing in a food processor and whizz until blended. Marinade the beef strips in the dressing until required.

When ready to serve, arrange the salad leaves on a large platter. Add the asparagus spears, tomatoes, peppers and quail eggs on top of the leaves. Season and drizzle with balsamic vinegar and olive oil. Top with the beef strips and Thai dressing, and serve immediately.

CAESAR SALAD

I adore this great American classic – if you want a more substantial meal, add some sliced, chargrilled chicken breast.

Serves 4

2 Romaine lettuces
1 ciabatta bread, roughly diced
6 tablespoons olive oil
2oz (50g) tin of anchovies
1 egg yolk
Juice 1 lemon
1 clove garlic, crushed
1 teaspoon mustard powder
Dash of Worcestershire sauce
Salt and pepper
2 oz (50g) Parmesan, grated

Preheat the oven to 180°C/Gas mark 4/Aga equivalent.

Lay the diced ciabatta on a baking tray, drizzle with olive oil and the crushed garlic and bake in a hot oven for about 10 minutes, or until golden brown. Drain on kitchen paper and allow to cool.

Remove the anchovies from the tin and place in a mixing bowl with about a teaspoon of the anchovy oil. Add the egg yolk, olive oil, lemon juice, mustard powder, Worcestershire sauce and seasoning and whisk together until you have a smooth dressing. Alternatively, place all the ingredients in a food processor and blitz for a few seconds.

Tear up the lettuces and arrange on a large platter. Add the diced ciabatta and pour over the dressing. Toss the salad, scatter over with Parmesan and serve immediately.

FRENCH BEANS WITH A DILL AND WALNUT DRESSING

Approx 2 lb (1 kg) French
 beans
4 shallots, finely chopped
3 tablespoons parsley,
 chopped
4 tablespoons fresh dill,
 chopped
3 tablespoons tarragon
 vinegar
Approx 5 fl oz (150ml) olive
 oil
4 oz (110g) chopped walnuts
Salt and pepper

Cook the beans in boiling water until just tender (do not overcook, the beans should still retain their bright colour). Drain and cool in a bowl of cold water until needed. Blend the remaining ingredients and season with salt and pepper. When ready to serve, remove the beans from the bowl and shake off any excess water. Arrange the beans on a platter, and pour the dressing over them.

SALAD NICOISE

This is a meal in itself, especially on a warm summer's evening. Serve with plenty of French bread or ciabatta.

Serves 4

4 Little Gem lettuces
4 hard boiled eggs
2 oz (50g) anchovies, drained from the tin
1 tin of tuna fish, drained
8-10 fresh black olives, stones removed

6 ripe tomatoes, cut into quarters
8 oz (225g) French green beans
12 waxy new potatoes, cooked and
 then cut in half
6-8 torn basil leaves

Vinaigrette Dressing:
5 tablespoons olive oil
1 tablespoon white wine vinegar
1 teaspoon caster sugar
1 teaspoon mustard powder
1 crushed garlic clove
Salt and pepper

Whisk all the dressing ingredients together.

Start by boiling the eggs in a saucepan of water, for about 10 minutes. Plunge in cold water and crack the shells. Boil the potatoes; when cooked, drain and cut in half – allow to cool before arranging in the salad. Cook the beans in boiling water for about 5 minutes and then drain and plunge into cold water. Leave until cool, then drain into a colander to dry off.

Tear up the lettuces and arrange on a platter. Break up the tuna with a fork and scatter over the lettuce. Add the French beans, anchovies, tomatoes and olives. Toss gently. Peel and quarter the hard-boiled eggs and arrange around the platter. Just before serving, add the dressing and tear some basil leaves over the salad.

WARM BACON AND AVOCADO SALAD

This would feed 4 as a starter or 2 as a main course.

9 oz (250g) streaky bacon, chopped
½ loaf 2 day old white bread, crusts removed
2 ripe avocados
2 Cos lettuces
Quantity of Wholegrain Mustard Dressing (see page 28)
Olive oil

First cut the bread into small cubes, place on a baking tray and drizzle with olive oil. Bake in a hot oven for about 10 minutes or until golden. Remove from oven and drain on some kitchen paper on a plate.

Fry the streaky bacon in some olive oil until crispy. Remove and drain on some kitchen paper. Roughly tear up the Cos lettuces and arrange on a large platter. Add the bacon and baked cubes of bread.

Quickly halve the avocados, remove stone and scoop out the flesh with a teaspoon (or peel from skin and slice). Add to the salad at the last minute or the avocados will go brown. Add the dressing and toss thoroughly. Serve immediately.

WARM CHICKEN (OR PHEASANT) SALAD

If you have access to plenty of pheasant, the breast is absolutely delicious in this recipe. We use pheasant as a substitute for chicken during the shooting season as the taste is far superior to any supermarket chicken.

Serves 4

4 skinless chicken or pheasant breasts
A mixture of crisp green lettuce leaves – Little Gem, Frisée, Romaine are ideal
5 rashers of back bacon, rinds removed
1 tablespoon olive oil
Juice of 1 lemon
1 tablespoon of chopped tarragon
Salt and pepper
A quantity of vinaigrette dressing (see page 39)

Slice the chicken or pheasant breasts into strips and the bacon into small pieces. Heat the oil in a large pan and add the strips and bacon pieces. Cook swiftly for 4-5 minutes (no longer). Add the lemon juice, tarragon, salt and pepper and cook for another 2 minutes.

In a large salad bowl, toss the salad in the vinaigrette dressing, add the chicken/pheasant and bacon and serve immediately.

Everybody helped at lambing

CHAPTER 4

Light Lunches

Sometimes you need something
more than a salad to fill the gap – the
following suggestions should help.

TANGY TOMATO TART

Perfect as a starter or light lunch.

Serves 6

500g pack ready-made puff pastry
8 large tomatoes, skinned, seeded and cut into wedges
1 teaspoon caster sugar
Salt and pepper

1 egg, beaten
9 oz (250g) mascarpone
4 oz (110g) Gorgonzola, chopped up
Small bunch flat leaf parsley, chopped

Preheat the oven to 200°C/Gas mark 6/Aga equivalent.

Roll out the pastry and cut into 6 rounds. Turn up the edges of the pastry slightly using the blade of a knife, as this will encourage the edges to rise evenly. Place the pastry circles onto a baking tray, and chill.

Season the chopped tomatoes with sugar and salt. Place in a sieve and allow them to drain for about 30 minutes.

Just before serving, brush the beaten egg around the edges of the pastry circles. Pile the drained tomatoes into the middle, about ½ inch (1.3cm) from the edge. Bake for about 20 minutes, or until the pastry has puffed up and is crisp and golden.

While the tart is baking, mix together the mascarpone and Gorgonzola. When the tarts are cooked, spoon a little onto each one and cook for a further 3 minutes, or until the cheese has warmed through.

Sprinkle each tart with the chopped parsley and a little freshly ground pepper. Serve immediately.

QUICHE LORRAINE

Real men will enjoy this quiche, I promise!

Serves 6

8 oz (225g) shortcrust pastry (see page 122)	2 eggs plus 1 egg yolk for brushing pastry base
9 oz (250g) streaky bacon, chopped	Salt and pepper
1 onion, chopped	4 oz (110g) Cheddar cheese, grated
5 fl oz (142ml carton) single cream	

Make the pastry, wrap in cling-film
and leave in the fridge for about an hour.

Preheat the oven to 200°C/Gas mark 6/Aga equivalent.

Fry the bacon in a little olive oil and add the onions after about 5 minutes. Cook until the bacon starts to get crispy and the onions are golden brown. Leave to one side. When the pastry has chilled sufficiently, roll out and line a 10 inch (25cm) loose-bottomed flan tin, about 2 inches (5cm) deep. Prick the base with a fork and place in a hot oven for about 10 minutes. When the pastry is just starting to go golden, take it out and brush with the beaten egg yolk. Return to the oven for 5-10 minutes, or until the base has a shiny glaze on it.

Remove from the oven and spread the base with the onion and bacon. Pour the cream into a small jug or bowl, add the 2 eggs and whisk with a fork. Add plenty of seasoning and then pour the mixture over the bacon. Sprinkle with grated cheese and bake for about 20-25 minutes or until the top is golden brown in colour. Serve with a crisp mixed salad and some French bread.

SMOKED TROUT AND DILL TARTLETS

Serves 6

1 lb (450g) shortcrust pastry (see page 122)
8 oz (225g) smoked trout (or salmon)
2 eggs plus 1 egg yolk for brushing onto the pastry base
2 tablespoons chopped dill, plus a little extra for decoration
10 fl oz (284ml carton) single cream
Watercress
Lemon wedges to garnish

6 tartlet tins

Preheat the oven to 200°C/Gas mark 6/Aga equivalent.

Roll the pastry onto a prepared surface and cut 6 circles to line the tartlet tins (4 inch (10cm) in diameter). Prick the bases with a fork and place the tins on a baking tray. Bake in a hot oven for about 5 minutes; remove from the oven and brush with a little beaten egg. Return to the oven for a further 5 minutes, or until the pastry is golden. Remove from the oven. Lower the oven temperature to 180°C/Gas mark 4.

Cut the trout into strips and divide equally into the 6 tartlets. Whisk the eggs in a bowl and add the chopped dill; whisk in the cream and season well. Pour the creamy mixture into the tartlets and bake for approximately 15 minutes, or until the tarts have set and the tops are golden. Serve hot or cold, with a little watercress on the side garnished with a lemon wedge and dill sprigs.

ROASTED PEPPER AND ONION TARTS

These tarts are very colourful and absolutely mouth-watering. Ideal for summer lunches or for picnics.

Serves 8

2 sheets ready made puff pastry, fresh or frozen
4 red peppers, de-seeded and 4 yellow peppers, de-seeded
2 onions
2 cloves garlic, chopped
2 courgettes
1 tablespoon sugar
1 teaspoon balsamic vinegar
Olive oil

First defrost the pastry if you're using a frozen packet.

Preheat oven to 200°C/Gas mark 6/Aga equivalent.

Slice the peppers and onions and place in a large roasting tin. Top and tail the courgettes and remove the outer skin. Using a potato peeler, peel the courgettes so that you have paper thin strips. Add to the peppers and onions. Scatter over the chopped garlic, sprinkle a tablespoon of sugar over the vegetables and a teaspoon of balsamic vinegar, and drizzle generously with olive oil. Roast for about 35-40 minutes or until the peppers, onions and courgettes beginning to go crispy round the edges. Allow to cool.

Roll out the puff pastry and using a saucer as a template, cut 8 circles. Prick each circle with a fork and lay out on a baking tray. Fill the centre of each circle with the pepper mix. Bake for about 10-15 minutes, or until the pastry is puffed up and golden brown.

GRANNY MAYNARD'S SAUSAGE PIE

Perfect for outdoor eating, whether you're at a Point-to-Point, out beating or just enjoying a lazy picnic. It is really a glorified sausage roll, but tastes so much better. As this has been passed down from my grandmother, I have had to guess at her quantities, but this seems to work OK.

Serves 6

1 lb (450g) good quality sausage meat. You could skin some
   sausages if you prefer, and for variety these could include
   pork and leek sausages.
Teaspoon dry mustard powder
8 oz (225g) shortcrust pastry (see page 122)
Pinch dried mixed herbs
Dash of Worcestershire sauce
Salt and pepper
1 egg (to glaze the pastry)

Preheat the oven to 180°C/Gas mark 4/Aga equivalent.

Place the sausage meat in a mixing bowl and season well with a teaspoon dried mustard powder, Worcestershire sauce, a pinch of dried mixed herbs and freshly ground salt and pepper.

Roll out half the pastry and line a 10 inch (25cm) metal flan tin. Add the sausage mixture. Roll out the remaining pastry – I like to use a lattice pastry cutter for the top, but you could interleave strips of pastry if you prefer. Cover the top of the pie and brush with beaten egg for a nice shiny glaze. Bake in a hot oven for 35-40 minutes or until golden brown.

Allow to cool before cutting into slices.

Variations:
Finely slice 2 leeks and fry gently in a little butter till soft. Mix in with the sausage meat and seasoning.
Roast some red and yellow peppers and add to the sausage meat.
Layer the sausage meat with sliced potatoes for a more substantial pie.

Play it again Sam

SPAGHETTI WITH PANCETTA, MUSHROOMS, ROCKET AND PARMESAN

This can be made in about 10 minutes flat. If you can't get pancetta use chopped streaky bacon instead.

Serves 4

9 oz (250g) pancetta
About 1 lb (450g) mushrooms (a mixture of chestnut, wild and large cap if possible)
3 cloves garlic, peeled and crushed
3 tablespoons olive oil
3 tablespoons balsamic vinegar
Juice of 1 lemon
1 bag of rocket leaves
3-4 handfuls shaved Parmesan
8 oz (225g) spaghetti

Bring a large pan of water to boil and add the pasta. When cooked, drain and return the pasta to the pan; remember to leave a small amount of water in the pan so that the pasta does not dry out.

Finely slice the mushrooms, discarding any woody bits. Fry the pancetta until crisp; remove and keep warm. Add half the olive oil to the pancetta fat and fry the mushrooms quickly with the garlic until golden, season well.

Remove from the heat and sprinkle with 1-2 tablespoons of lemon juice and the vinegar. Add the contents of the pan to the cooked spaghetti; add the rocket, remaining olive oil and half the Parmesan shavings. Toss well, season and transfer to a warmed serving dish; scatter with the remaining Parmesan shavings.

SALMON FISH CAKES

I love fish cakes and always choose them when I see them on the menu. If you don't have fresh salmon available you could use a good quality tinned variety.

Serves 4

4 salmon steaks or 2 tins of salmon, drained
1 lb (450g) potatoes, peeled and diced
2 tablespoons chopped parsley
4 spring onions, finely chopped
Juice of 1 lemon
1 tablespoon capers (optional)
Salt and pepper
¼ pint (150ml) milk
2 oz (50g) butter
4 oz (110g) breadcrumbs (use day old white bread, blast in a
    food processor and bake in a hot oven for about 10
    minutes. Blast again until it looks like sand!)
Seasoned flour
2 eggs, beaten
3 tablespoons cooking oil

Place the potatoes in a large saucepan of salted water. Bring to the boil and simmer until they are cooked through. Drain in a colander and return to the pan. Add the butter and milk and mash until smooth.

Gently fry the salmon steaks in a pan for a few minutes each side until the fish begins to flake. Remove from the pan and flake, removing any skin and bones. Add the flaked fish to the potato mash; add the chopped parsley, capers (optional), lemon juice and finely chopped spring onion, and season well. Place in the fridge until cold (this makes it easier to shape). When ready to cook, use your hands to shape the mix into small cakes (you need about 8). Roll in seasoned flour; dip in the beaten egg and then coat with breadcrumbs. Shallow fry in a little oil until golden on both sides. Serve with tartare sauce (or crème fraîche mixed with some capers) or salsa, and a crisp green salad.

SPECIAL CURRY SAUCE

My mother uses this sauce for making her famous curries. It is very versatile and can be used with any cooked meat (e.g. lamb, pork or chicken) or prawns. It is also delicious with hard-boiled eggs, cooked diced potatoes and lightly cooked cauliflower florets as a vegetarian alternative. Serve with a selection of side dishes and a large bowl of cooked rice.

Serves 4

2 tablespoons of either a top quality ready made curry powder or, ideally, make it yourself:

Homemade Garam Masala:
½ teaspoon ginger
½ teaspoon turmeric
1 teaspoon chilli powder
1 teaspoon cumin
1½ teaspoons paprika
1 teaspoon ground coriander

4 oz (110g) block creamed coconut dissolved in 10 fl oz
    (275ml) boiling water or 1 tin coconut milk
1 large onion, chopped
1 tablespoon vegetable oil
1 eating apple, peeled, cored and chopped
Juice of 1 lemon or lime
150g carton natural yoghurt

Gently fry the onion in a little vegetable oil until soft. Add

the spices or ready made curry powder, the chopped apple, lemon or lime juice, coconut block or milk and finally the yoghurt (a little at a time to prevent curdling). Simmer gently for about 15 minutes or until the sauce has reduced a little.

CHICKEN CURRY

I love curry lunches – it's a great way of entertaining in an informal way. Double or triple the recipe accordingly.

Serves 4

1 quantity of curry sauce (see page 50)
Shredded meat from one small cooked chicken
Approx 10 oz (275g) Basmati rice
Selection of side dishes
1 packet poppadums

Put the curry sauce in a casserole dish and add the cooked chicken. Simmer gently until the meat is piping hot.

Serve with a platter of cooked white rice and a selection of side dishes.
These could include chopped tomato, chopped cucumber, chopped peppers, cashew nuts, grated coconut, sliced bananas (must be done at the last minute or they will go brown) – but use your imagination! Offer some really good chutneys, both mild and hot, and no curry is complete without a huge plate of poppadums. You can now buy these ready cooked which saves time.

Serve only the best quality Basmati rice – it is far superior to anything else.
I find that one large serving spoon of uncooked rice feeds two people and weighs about 2oz (50g). Add a bit more for second helpings, but this way you should get the quantities just about right. The last thing you need is a mountain of leftover rice. Cook the rice following directions on the packet (or cook in your usual way). Transfer to a serving dish and cover with some foil; keep warm until needed.

Vegetarian version:
Lightly cook a variety of vegetables, e.g. cauliflower, broccoli, potato, diced carrots. Add to the curry sauce and gently simmer till the vegetables have cooked through and are piping hot.

CHAPTER 5

Vegetables

I've included some of my
favourite vegetable recipes.
Some are meals in themselves;
others compliment most meat and
fish dishes.

RATATOUILLE

This classic French vegetable 'stew' is, I think, more delicious eaten cold, or maybe just slightly warm. Ideally leave for a few hours before serving to allow the flavours to develop.

Serves 4-6

1 onion cut into chunks
2 red peppers (de-seeded), each pepper cut into about 6 chunks
4 courgettes, diced
1 aubergine, diced
1 lb (450g) ripe tomatoes, chopped
4 tablespoons olive oil

2 cloves garlic, chopped
Bunch basil leaves
Olives (optional)
1-2 tins chopped tomatoes (if using traditional version)
Salt and pepper

I have become addicted to roasting vegetables and rarely cook them any other way, but there is the traditional method of cooking ratatouille if you prefer.

Roasted Version

Preheat oven to 200°C/Gas mark 6/Aga equivalent.

Lay out the vegetables in a roasting tin and drizzle about 4 tablespoons of best quality olive oil. Scatter over the chopped garlic and a good bunch of basil leaves; give everything a good mix with your hands so that it's coated with olive oil and season well with salt and pepper. Roast in a very hot oven for about 35-45 minutes or until the vegetables start to go brown at the edges. Just before serving, you could scatter over some olives.

Traditional Version

Fry the onions and garlic in a fairly generous amount of good quality olive oil (about 4 tablespoons). Gradually add the aubergine, courgettes and red peppers, one after the other, allowing a few minutes for each vegetable to cook on its own. Finally add the tomatoes and basil leaves (you could use a mixture of both fresh and tinned tomatoes, but I would definitely put in at least 1 tin of chopped tomatoes). Season well and cook for a further 25 minutes on a low heat until the vegetables are soft, but not mushy.

BRAISED RED CABBAGE

This is the perfect accompaniment to most winter dishes and its glossy red colour compliments any carrots or beans you may also wish to serve.

Serves 6

1 small red cabbage
1 onion, chopped
1 clove garlic, chopped
1 cooking apple, peeled, cored and sliced
3 tablespoons white wine vinegar
3 tablespoons water
1 oz (25g) brown sugar
2 oz (50g) butter
Salt and pepper

Shred the cabbage either by hand or in a food processor.

Melt the butter in a casserole pan and add the onion and garlic. Fry for a few minutes and then add the apple slices and shredded cabbage. Add the water, vinegar and sugar and stir until everything has mixed in. Season with salt and pepper and simmer gently for about 35-40 minutes. Serve straight from the casserole pan, it doesn't need draining.

HERBY PUY LENTILS

These are good and hearty, and would go well with bangers and mash.

Serves 4

9 oz (250g) Puy lentils (any other kind of lentil will go too soft)
1 onion, peeled and finely chopped
1 clove garlic, peeled and crushed
1 tablespoon olive oil
Dash of Worcestershire sauce
Salt and pepper
Tablespoon tomato purée
2 large tomatoes, skinned, de-seeded and chopped
1 bay leaf
Assortment of fresh herbs, about a tablespoon of each, e.g. rosemary, oregano – whatever is available
1 glass red wine
Approximately ¼ – ½ pint (150-275ml) vegetable stock
¼ teaspoon chilli powder – if you like a bit of spice!

Gently fry the onion and garlic in the olive oil until soft; if using chilli powder, add that and fry for 1 minute. Add the rest of the ingredients and enough stock to cover the lentils. Bring slowly to the boil and then cook very gently for 1 hour. Top up with more stock if necessary. Season to taste and serve as an accompaniment with any meat dish.

A spot of decorating

POTATO GRATIN

This is another good old standby, and goes with just about everything.

Serves 6

2½ lb (1 kg) white potatoes (I use Desirée), peeled and sliced
½ pint (275ml) milk
1 bay leaf
10 fl oz (284ml carton) double cream
2 onions
2 sprigs rosemary, chopped
2 cloves garlic, peeled and chopped
2 oz (50g) butter
Salt and pepper
1 oz (25g) Parmesan

Preheat oven to 180°C/Gas mark 4/Aga equivalent.

Pour the milk and cream into a pan, add the bay leaf and one onion, peeled and halved, and slowly heat up until it has almost reached boiling point. Remove and allow to infuse for 10 minutes.

Meanwhile, arrange half the potato slices in a layer over the base of a buttered ovenproof dish. Finely slice the remaining onion and scatter over the potatoes, with some of the chopped rosemary. Add another layer of potato slices, scatter over the remaining rosemary and strain the infused milk and cream mix over the potatoes. Season with salt and pepper, grate the Parmesan over the top and dot with butter. Bake in a moderate oven for about an hour, or until crisp and golden.

ROASTED DICED POTATOES

I like this method of roasting potatoes. It doesn't take long and is just a bit healthier than normal roast potatoes

Serves 4-6

Approx 2 lb (900g) potatoes, peeled and diced
3 cloves garlic, chopped
Olive oil
Handful chopped rosemary
Teaspoon sea salt

Preheat oven to 200°C/Gas mark 6/Aga equivalent.

Dry the diced potatoes with some kitchen paper towel and place in a roasting tin. Sprinkle over the chopped rosemary, sea salt and garlic and drizzle with olive oil. Mix with your hands until the potatoes are covered with the oil, and roast in a hot oven for about 35 minutes, or until the potatoes are golden brown and crunchy.

BUBBLE AND SQUEAK

Cabbage and potatoes may sound like an odd combination, but it is delicious dish to serve with a plateful of sausages.

Serves 4

1½ lb (700g) potatoes, peeled
1 Savoy cabbage, shredded
1 small onion, finely chopped
2 oz (50g) butter
About ¼ pint (150ml) milk
4 oz (110g) Cheddar cheese, grated
Salt and pepper

Preheat the oven to 200°C/Gas mark 6/Aga equivalent.

Place the peeled potatoes in a large pan of salted water, bring to the boil and cook for about 25 minutes or until done. Drain and mash with plenty of butter and milk. Season with salt and pepper. Cook the shredded cabbage in a small amount of boiling water for about 3 minutes – do not overcook! Drain and add to the mashed potato. Add the chopped onion and give everything a good stir. Place in an ovenproof dish and sprinkle with plenty of Cheddar cheese. Bake in a hot oven for about 30 minutes, or until golden brown.

SPINACH GRATIN

Serves 4

1 bag frozen chopped spinach
1 onion, chopped
1 oz (25g) butter
1 tablespoon flour
½ pint (275ml) milk
Salt and pepper
Worcestershire sauce
1 teaspoon wholegrain mustard
4 oz (110g) Cheddar cheese, grated

Preheat the oven to 180°C/Gas mark 4/Aga equivalent.

Gently cook the spinach in a dash of water for a few minutes. Drain thoroughly, squeezing out any excess water.

Melt the butter, add the chopped onion and cook for a few minutes until the onion has softened. Add the flour to form a paste. Gradually add the milk and cook until the sauce has thickened. Season with salt, pepper, mustard and a dash of Worcestershire sauce. Add the spinach to the onion sauce and mix well. Place in a gratin dish and sprinkle with grated Cheddar cheese. Cook in the oven for about 15 minutes or until the cheese is bubbling and golden brown.

BAKED AUBERGINE

This is dead easy to make and can be served either hot or cold, as a vegetable dish or salad.

Serves 4-6

2 medium aubergine
¼ pint (150ml) olive oil
1 clove garlic, crushed
1 teaspoon marjoram or thyme
2½ oz (60g) freshly grated Parmesan
8 oz (225g) tomatoes, sliced into thin rounds, sufficient for each aubergine slice
Salt and pepper

Preheat the oven to 220°C/Gas mark 7/Aga equivalent.

Chop off the ends of the aubergine, and then cut slices about ½ inch (2.5cm) thick. Mix together the oil, garlic, herbs and seasoning. Liberally brush with olive oil onto both sides of the aubergine slice, and place on a baking dish in a single layer. Bake in a hot oven for about 12 minutes. Remove from the oven and sprinkle with Parmesan. Place a slice of tomato over each aubergine slice and return to the oven for a further 10-15 minutes. Transfer the aubergine slices onto a platter and either serve hot or allow to cool.

STUFFED MARROW

I only make this once a year, when our courgettes have turned into marrows. Despite the fact that everyone thinks they don't like marrow, they love eating this. What you don't get is a horrible, watery mush – instead, the marrow is almost 'al dente' when cooked, which is most acceptable. It's the perfect supper dish if you have some left over ragout when making spaghetti bolognese. Alternatively, use a quality jar of bought ragout.

Serves 4

1 medium marrow (not an absolute monster, please)
Bowlful of left over ragout (or a bought jar if nothing is left over)
8 oz (225g) long grain rice
½ pint (275ml) milk
1 oz (25g) butter
Tablespoon plain flour
4 oz (110g) mature Cheddar cheese
Salt and pepper
Dash of Worcestershire sauce

Preheat the oven to 180°C/Gas mark 4/Aga equivalent.

If the marrow is not too old it does not need peeling, but do wash it first to remove any mud! Cut in half, scoop out the seeds and set aside.

Cook the rice, mix it in with the ragout sauce and heat through. To make the white sauce, melt the butter in a pan, add the flour and mix to a paste. Gradually add the milk and stir thoroughly until smooth. Season with salt and pepper and a dash of Worcestershire sauce. Place the rice mixture inside the two scooped out marrows and pour on the white sauce. Sprinkle with the grated Cheddar cheese and bake for about 25-30 minutes, or until golden brown.

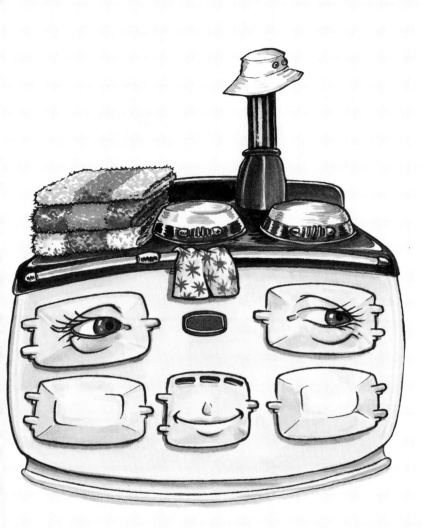

Jolly hols

HOMEMADE PESTO

If you grow your own basil this is lovely to make throughout the summer.

3 handfuls basil leaves
1 clove garlic
3½ oz (100g) bag of pinenuts
4 oz (110g) freshly grated Parmesan
Approx ¼ pint (150ml) olive oil
Salt and pepper

I tend to use my food processor for this, but you could use a pestle and mortar if you prefer.

Blitz the basil, garlic, Parmesan and pinenuts for a few seconds. Gradually add the olive oil until you have the right consistency. Season with salt and pepper and keep in the fridge until you need it.

For a delicious pasta supper for 2, add some single cream or crème fraîche to about 4 tablespoons pesto. Cook some tagliatelle, drain and return to the pan. Add the creamy pesto and serve with extra Parmesan sprinkled on top.

Alternatives:
Use fresh parsley instead of basil
Walnuts can replace pinenuts

CHAPTER 6

Teatime Treats

My grandmother
knew how to bake cakes and I seem
to have inherited her love of baking. What
gives me even more pleasure is that our girls
love baking too. Here are some all time classics.

BANANA BREAD

Our family love bananas, but are very fussy and only like them when they're still a bit green. So you can imagine what happens when they start to ripen – no one touches them with a barge pole. I'm usually left with a reasonable quantity of no-good bananas, which is where this recipe comes in! Like gingerbread, this improves with age and I suggest it's better to eat a few days after baking. I happen to like more fruit in banana bread so this includes sultanas and dates.

8 oz (225g) self-raising flour
4 oz (110g) softened butter
4 very ripe bananas, mashed
6 oz (175g) soft, brown sugar
2 oz (50g) chopped walnuts
2 oz (50g) sultanas
2 oz (50g) chopped dates
2 eggs, beaten

1 lb loaf tin, greased and lined

Preheat the oven to 170°C/Gas mark 3/Aga equivalent.

First mash the bananas in a bowl. In another bowl, sift in the flour first, and then add the eggs, butter and mashed bananas and mix well (if using a food processor, whizz for 10 seconds). Fold in the dried fruit and walnuts until everything is nicely mixed together. Pour into the prepared loaf tin. Bake for 40-45 minutes. Turn out onto a wire rack to cool.

LEMON DRIZZLE CAKE

This cake will disappear within seconds – so enjoy it while it lasts!

6 oz (175g) caster sugar
6 oz (175g) butter, softened
6 oz (175g) self raising flour, sifted
3 eggs
Zest of 1 lemon
Approx. 4 tablespoons milk

For the syrup:
Juice of 2 lemons
4 oz (110g) icing
   sugar

1 lb loaf tin, greased and lined (I use convenient paper inserts, available from cookshops).

Preheat the oven to 180°C/Gas mark 4/Aga equivalent.

Cream together the sugar and butter and beat in the eggs a little at a time. Add the lemon zest. Gently fold in the flour and add the milk. Pour into the prepared tin and bake for about 30-35 minutes or until risen and golden on top (test with a skewer: if it comes out clean, it is done).

While it is cooking, make the syrup. Place the lemon juice and sugar in a saucepan and heat gently until the sugar has dissolved.

When the cake is ready and still hot from the oven, prick all over with a skewer and pour over the syrup. You need to allow enough time for the cake to have absorbed all the syrup before serving. It is much easier to cut into slices when allowed to cool properly.

Baking day

DARK STICKY GINGERBREAD

Weighing treacle is a messy business. My method is to dip a large tablespoon into a mug of hot water, dry quickly and then spoon out the treacle so that it glides out easily. This cake is best left for a day or two before eating, as the longer you leave it the stickier it gets.

4 oz (110g) butter
About 4-5 tablespoons of black treacle (½ small tin)
2-3 tablespoons of golden syrup
¼ pint (150ml) milk
2 large eggs, beaten
8 oz (225g) plain flour
2 oz (50g) caster sugar
1 teaspoon mixed spice
1 teaspoon bicarbonate of soda
4 teaspoons ground ginger

Preheat the oven to 170°C/Gas mark 3/Aga equivalent.

Grease an 8 inch (20cm) square cake tin and line the bottom and sides with parchment paper. Put the butter, treacle and syrup in a saucepan and heat gently until the butter has melted. Remove from the heat and add the milk. When the mixture has cooled slightly, add the eggs. Sieve the dry ingredients into a mixing bowl and add the treacle mixture, beating everything together. Pour into the prepared tin and bake in a moderate oven for 50 minutes to 1 hour. Turn out of tin and leave to cool on a wire rack. When cold, wrap up in tin foil or put into an airtight tin. Leave for a few days!

ALMOND AND LEMON CAKE

I like serving this more as a pudding than a cake. Scatter some raspberries over the top, dust with icing sugar and serve with vanilla ice cream.

8 oz (225g) softened butter
8 oz (225g) caster sugar
4 large eggs
2 tablespoons plain flour
8 oz (225g) ground almonds
½ teaspoon almond essence
Zest and juice of 2 lemons

Preheat the oven to 180°C/Gas mark 4/Aga equivalent.

Cream together the sugar and butter until very soft; beat in the eggs a little at a time (adding a little sifted flour after each time to prevent any curdling). Stir in the ground almonds, zest and lemon juice and almond essence and pour into a cake tin (I use an 8 inch (20cm) square tin, lined with parchment paper). Bake for about 35-45 minutes – the top should be firm when it's done, but keep an eye on it to prevent it from burning, and if it needs a little longer, cover the top with foil.

Leave to cool for about 10 minutes before turning out on a wire rack. Once completely cold, wrap in foil and ideally leave for a day or two before eating.

CHOCOLATE BROWNIES

These American brownies are a family favourite – with a slight crunch on top and then deliciously squidgy inside, they don't hang around for long.

3 large eggs
10 oz (275g) caster sugar
3 oz (75g) butter, melted
½ teaspoon pure vanilla extract
4 oz (110g) plain flour

4 tablespoons cocoa powder
½ teaspoon baking powder
Pinch of salt
4 oz (110g) chopped walnuts

Preheat the oven to 180°C/Gas mark 4/Aga equivalent.

Grease and line an 8 inch (20cm) square cake tin. Whisk the eggs and the sugar together until the mixture is thick and creamy. Beat in the melted butter and vanilla extract. In another bowl, sieve the flour, cocoa, baking powder and salt and then fold the dry ingredients into the creamy mixture, adding the walnuts last. Ensure that everything is well mixed and pour into the prepared tin. Bake for around 35 to 40 minutes and then allow to cool for around 10 minutes before cutting into squares.

P.S. For a delicious, calorific pudding serve these with some good quality vanilla ice cream and pour over hot chocolate fudge sauce. It will disappear in a trice.

Hot Chocolate Fudge Sauce
2oz (50g) butter, 3 tablespoons golden syrup and 3 tablespoons cocoa powder.

In a saucepan, mix all the ingredients together and simmer gently for about 3 minutes. Pour immediately over the ice cream and brownies.

ZUCCHINI BREAD

If you've never tried this, give it a go – it's delicious!

Makes 2 loaves

8 oz (225g) self-raising flour
8 oz (225g) soft brown sugar
3 teaspoons cinnamon
1 teaspoon salt
3 courgettes, shredded
¼ pint (150ml) sunflower oil
1 teaspoon vanilla extract
3 eggs, beaten

Preheat the oven to 180°C/Gas mark 4/ Aga equivalent.

In a mixing bowl, whisk together the eggs and oil and then stir in all the other ingredients (it looks a little odd at this stage – more like a batter!). Pour into two 1 lb loaf tins (lined with paper inserts) and bake for about 40 minutes or until golden brown. Leave in their tins for about 10 minutes before turning out onto wire racks. Allow to cool before cutting into slices. Spread with butter if you prefer.

THE ULTIMATE CHOCOLATE CAKE

I always use the all in one method for making sponge cakes; it saves time and washing up. You can either place all the ingredients in a large mixing bowl (make sure the butter is really soft) and whisk everything together, or use a food processor.

This chocolate cake is one that I use for birthdays and simply when I feel like eating something totally indulgent. The chocolate drops are optional but I like using them as they add to the overall chocolatey effect.

5 eggs, beaten
8 oz (225g) self-raising flour, sieved
1 teaspoon baking powder, sieved
10 oz (275g) softened butter
10 oz (275g) caster sugar
2 oz (50g) cocoa powder, sieved
1–2 tablespoons milk, if necessary
1 packet of plain chocolate drops (optional)

Two 9 inch (23cm) round non-stick sandwich tins, greased and lined.

Beat 5 eggs.

Mix all ingredients.

Preheat the oven to 180°C/Gas mark 4/Aga equivalent.

Place all the ingredients (except the chocolate drops) in a food processor and whizz for about 10 seconds. Add a tablespoon or two of milk to achieve a slightly floppy consistency. Fold in the chocolate drops and then pour into the prepared tins.

Alternatively, sieve the dry ingredients into a large mixing bowl, add the remaining ingredients and beat or whisk until smooth.

Bake for about 25-35 minutes – if anything, I take the cake out when still very slightly underdone. Allow to cool a little before turning out onto wire racks. If you like your cake to absorb the icing, prick holes over the bottom cake and add half the icing while it's still warm. Spread the remaining icing all over the top and around the sides.

Rich Chocolate Icing

6oz (175g) quality dark chocolate
   (minimum 70% cocoa solids)
8 oz (225g) butter
2 oz (50g) cocoa powder, sifted
10 oz (275g) icing sugar, sifted

First melt the chocolate, either in a
microwave or in a bowl standing in a
saucepan of simmering water (if you have
an Aga, it melts wonderfully in the
simmering oven). Beat the butter until it
is soft and creamy and then add the
melted chocolate, sifted cocoa powder
and icing sugar, and whisk
thoroughly until glossy and smooth.

Add chocolate drops.

Bake for 30-40 minutes –
test with skewer.

Make icing and decorate.

Serve!

CARROT CAKE

I got addicted to carrot cake when we lived in Australia – for some reason I'd never tasted it until then, and now it's one of my top 10 favourite cakes.

6 oz (175g) self-raising flour
6 oz (175g) wholemeal self-raising flour
6 oz (175g) light muscavado sugar
1 teaspoon cinnamon
4 eggs, beaten
7 fl oz (200ml) sunflower oil
3 medium carrots, peeled and grated
Juice and zest of 1 orange
4 oz (110g) walnuts
1 banana, mashed

Icing
7 oz (200g) tub cream cheese
4 oz (110g) icing sugar, sifted
Zest of 1 lemon

Preheat the oven to 180°C/Gas mark 4/Aga equivalent.

Whisk the eggs and the oil together, and stir in the rest of the ingredients. Pour into a prepared square 8 inch (20cm) baking tin. Bake for about an hour (it may take a bit longer depending on your oven) – when it's risen and firm, it's ready. Cool slightly before turning out onto a wire rack.

To make the icing, whisk together the cream cheese, icing sugar and the lemon zest until smooth. Spread over the cooled cake and cut into slices.

QUICK MADEIRA CAKE

8 oz (225g) self-raising flour
1 teaspoon baking powder
6 oz (175g) caster sugar
6 oz (175g) softened butter
Grated zest and juice of 1 lemon
3 large eggs
2 tablespoons milk

Preheat the oven to 170°C/Gas mark 3/Aga equivalent.

Sift the flour and baking powder into a mixing bowl and add the other ingredients. Mix together with a wooden spoon or use an electric mixer (1 minute only) until the mixture is creamy. Pour into a 1 lb loaf tin, greased and lined, sprinkle with a little extra caster sugar and bake for about an hour. Test with a skewer, if it comes out clean it is done. Cool before turning out onto a wire rack.

Variations
Add any of the following to the mixture:
6 oz (175g) glacé cherries, or
2 oz (50g) dessicated coconut.
Zest and juice of 1 orange or lime instead of lemon juice.
For a nuttier taste, replace 4 oz (110g) flour with ground almonds (or finely chopped walnuts, hazelnuts or pecans).

GLACE FRUIT CAKE

If you're not a great fan of dark fruit cakes this will suit you down to the ground, and indeed this is the cake my mother-in-law bakes as our Christmas cake. Use a variety of glacé fruit for the most delicious cake imaginable.

12 oz (350g) plain flour, sifted
2 teaspoons baking powder
6 oz (175g) ground almonds
12 oz (350g) caster sugar
12 oz (350g) softened butter

4 large eggs
12 oz (350g) chopped mixed glacé fruit (pineapple, cherries, and angjelica for example)
4 oz (110g) chopped brazil nuts

Grease and line an 8 inch (20cm) square cake tin or a 9 inch (23cm) round deep cake tin.

Preheat the oven to 140°C/Gas mark 1/Aga equivalent.

Sift the flour and baking powder into a large mixing bowl, add the ground almonds, sugar, softened butter and eggs. Mix together with a wooden spoon for a few minutes before using an electric mixer or food processor (do not over-mix in the processor). Add the chopped glacé fruit and nuts and mix thoroughly.

Spoon the mixture into the prepared tin and spread evenly over the base and into the corners. Give the tin a few sharp taps to level the mixture and make a slight depression in the centre of the cake.

Bake in the centre of the oven for about 2½ – 2¾ hours. Test the cake by pressing the centre with a finger – it should feel firm and springy when cooked.

Leave to cool in the tin, then turn out onto a wire rack. Wrap the cake in foil and store in a cool place for up to a week before decorating.

SPECIAL ALMOND PASTE FOR FRUIT CAKE

As I love marzipan but not the icing, this is the bit I nibble away at!

8 oz (225g) ground almonds
6 oz (175g) caster sugar
4 oz (110g) icing sugar
1 egg
1 tablespoon lemon juice
1 tablespoon brandy or sherry
2 drops almond essence

Mix together the caster sugar and sifted icing sugar in a mixing bowl. In a small bowl, whisk the egg with the lemon juice and other flavourings and add to the sugar mix. Add the almonds and mix everything together until you have a dough-type mix. Using your hands, knead until smooth. Sift some icing sugar onto a board and roll out the paste to the required shape of the cake. Allow to dry before icing the cake.

LEMON CURD CAKE

This lemon curd filling makes a delicious alternative to jam in the classic Victoria Sponge Sandwich Cake.

4 eggs, beaten
8 oz (225g) self raising flour, sifted
8 oz (225g) caster sugar
8 oz (225g) softened butter
2-3 tablespoons milk
Icing Sugar

Preheat the oven to 170°C/Gas mark 3/Aga equivalent.

Use the all-in-one method. Place all the ingredients, except the lemon curd, in a large mixing bowl and whisk everything together. Alternatively whizz for about 10 seconds in a food processor. (If using a food processor, always aerate the flour first for a few seconds by removing the funnel to let the air in and pulse for a couple of seconds.)

Spread the mixture into two 8 inch (20cm) sandwich tins, greased and lined, and bake for around 30-35 minutes, or until the centres feel springy to the touch. Allow to rest for 5 minutes before turning onto wire racks. When cool, sandwich the cakes with lemon curd and lightly dust the top of the cake with icing sugar.

Lemon Curd:
3 oz (75g) caster sugar
Grated zest and juice of 1 large juicy lemon
2 eggs
2 oz (50g) unsalted butter

Melt the butter on a very gentle heat and then add all the other ingredients and stir gently until the mixture becomes thick. Do not allow to boil or you will end up with scrambled

CHILDRENS' YUMMY KRISPIES

7 oz (200g) each of:
Marshmallows
Toffees
Butter
Rice Krispies

Melt the marshmallows, toffees and butter together slowly in pan, and then add the Rice Krispies. Pour into a lined Swiss roll tin and refrigerate. Cut into squares when cool.

Tea and sympathy

COFFEE WALNUT CAKE

I make no apologies for yet another all in one cake – the truth is that it is so easy to make and takes no longer than 10 minutes to assemble.

8 oz (225g) self raising flour, sifted by hand or in a processor
1 teaspoon baking powder
8 oz (225g) caster sugar
8 oz (225g) softened butter
4 eggs
Dash of milk
4 oz (110g) chopped walnuts
1 tablespoon strong instant coffee, dissolved with 1 tablespoon boiling water

Preheat the oven to 180°C/Gas mark 4/Aga equivalent.

Mix all the ingredients (except the walnuts) in a bowl and whisk thoroughly, or use a food processor (see previous cake recipes). Add a drop of milk to achieve the right dropping consistency. Then fold in the walnuts and mix well. Pour into two prepared 8 inch (20cm) sandwich tins and bake for about 25-40 minutes. When cool, turn onto wire racks.

Coffee Icing
6 oz (175g) softened butter
4 oz (110g) sifted icing sugar
1 tablespoon of coffee essence (make as above)
Walnut halves to decorate – about 10

If using a processor, you can sift the icing sugar by whizzing it for a few seconds before adding the rest of the ingredients (anything to avoid sifting icing sugar – 9 times out of 10 I end up with a cloud of sugar in my face!). Whizz together until creamy. Sandwich the cakes together and spread the remaining icing on top. Decorate with halved walnuts.

FLAPJACKS WITH A DIFFERENCE

Crispy AND chewy – this is the ultimate flapjack!

8 oz (225g) butter
2 tablespoons golden syrup
8 oz (225g) soft brown sugar
4 oz (110g) self-raising flour
4 oz (110g) porridge oats
6 oz (175g) cornflakes

Line a Swiss roll tin with parchment paper

Preheat the oven to 200°C/Gas mark 6/Aga equivalent.

In a pan, melt the butter and syrup and then add the remaining ingredients. Stir until well mixed, then pour into the prepared Swiss roll tin and bake for about 10-15 minutes or until just golden in colour. Cool and then cut into squares or fingers.

SCONES

What could be more indulgent than a good old-fashioned cream tea? These scones need to be filled with fresh cream and strawberry jam and eaten when warm.

8 oz (225g) self-raising flour
1 oz (25g) butter
1 egg
¼ pint (150ml) milk
Pinch salt

Preheat the oven to 220°C/Gas mark 7/Aga equivalent.

Sift the flour into a bowl and rub in the butter until it resembles breadcrumbs. Make a well in the centre of the flour, add the beaten egg and a little of the milk. Mix together until you have a soft dough, adding more milk if necessary.

Roll out onto a floured board and knead it very lightly into a circle. Roll the dough to at least 1 inch (2.5cm) thick (I've learnt the hard way, and believe me, an inch thickness is what you need). Use a 2 inch (5cm) pastry cutter to stamp out the circles. Place on a greased baking tray and bake in a hot oven for about 10 minutes, or until the scones are well risen and golden. Cool on a wire rack but serve while still warm, splitting them in half and piling on the cream and jam. Scones do not keep well, so you'll just have to eat them then and there. There are times in life when you have to make some sacrifices!

LOUISA'S CHOCOLATE CHIP COOKIES

These are fabulous cookies – crispy on the outside and gently chewy in the middle.

8 oz (225g) self-raising flour
4 oz (110g) caster sugar
4 oz (110g) butter
A little milk
1 packet (100g) chocolate chips
2 teaspoons cinnamon
Grated rind 2 oranges

Makes approximately 9 large cookies/16 small cookies.

Preheat the oven to 180°C/Gas mark 4/Aga equivalent.

Place the flour, sugar, butter and cinnamon a mixing bowl. Rub in the butter with your fingertips and add the chocolate chips and orange zest. Bind together with a little milk to form a firm dough (flour your hands first as the mixture can be very sticky). Using your hands, roll lumps of the mixture into approx. 3 inch (7cm) balls. Place on a lightly floured baking tray and flatten using the palm of your hand. Bake for about 15 minutes or until golden – check half way through the cooking, as you may have to turn around the tray to prevent the back cookies getting over-cooked. Place on a baking tray to cool.

Mix the ingredients. Flour, warm water, yeast and salt.

Knead until it is smooth and springy.

Put in a warm place to rise to twice its size.

Once it has risen, knock back to remove the air.

Divide the dough into baking tins and allow to rise again.

Bake the loaves until they sound hollow when tapped ... then eat!

CHAPTER 7

Homemade Bread

There is nothing quite so impressive as a loaf of homemade bread – the aroma wafts around the kitchen and makes me think that I could quite happily make bread all day long. I first learnt how to make bread when I lived in Mongolia – the local bread was rock hard, and although the flour we used was nothing special, at least we had slightly more palatable bread to eat.

Since you could argue that bread making takes up a lot of time, I think it's worth making double the amount each time and freezing the rest. Actually, it doesn't take that long to make, and you can get on with your life while the dough is rising. If you work during the week, this is especially good to make at the weekend, when you can catch up with reading the papers while the dough is rising.

This quantity makes 2 x 1lb (450g) loaves

1 packet (3 lb/1.35 kilos) strong white flour (Canadian flour is very good) – but choose what you like
2 sachets easy-blend dried yeast
4 teaspoons salt
4 oz (110g) butter or lard
About 1 pint (570 ml) hand hot water, i.e. you should be able to dip your finger in the water and hold it for a few seconds – it must not scald!

Tip the flour into a large mixing bowl, mix in the butter with your hands, add the salt and the dried yeast, and give it a good stir. Add the hot water a little at a time, and start mixing with a spoon until it's easier to use your hands. If it's looking a little dry, add a touch more water; if too sticky, a little more flour. When the mixture has formed into a large doughy ball, place on a lightly floured surface and knead for 5-10 minutes, until the dough is smooth and elastic.

Return to the mixing bowl (washed first in hot water, dried and lightly oiled), cover with cling film and leave in a warm place to double in size.

Preheat the oven to 220°C/Gas mark 7/Aga equivalent.

Once the dough has doubled in size you have the fun of 'knocking down' – literally, punching the dough with your fist to let the air out. It is then ready to place in the loaf tins. Cover again and allow to have a second rise or 'prove' for about half an hour, or until puffy.

Remove the covering. If you want a crusty top, sprinkle the dough with cold water just before placing in the oven. If you like a soft-top, dust a little flour over the top instead. Or you can just leave it as it is. Cook in a hot oven for about 30-40 minutes. To check if it's ready, turn the bread out of the tins and knock on the bottom of the loaf – if it sounds hollow, it's done. If the bread needs further cooking, return to the oven for 5-10 minutes, but turn the loaves upside down so that the base gets a chance to crisp up. When satisfied that it is properly cooked, turn out onto wire racks and allow to cool.

FOCACCIA

This delicious Italian bread is a doddle to make and tastes divine.

1½lb (700g) strong white flour
1 sachet easy-blend dried yeast
Approx ½ pint (275ml) hand
    hot water
1 tablespoon olive oil
2 teaspoons salt

Several sprigs rosemary
1 small red onion, chopped
2-3 sun dried tomatoes,
    chopped
4 oz (110g) streaky bacon,
    chopped
1 teaspoon sea salt

Sift the flour and add the salt, yeast and olive oil. Add the water and mix well until you have a ball of dough. Knead well and leave to rise until doubled in size. While the bread is rising, fry the bacon in a little olive oil, add the onion, and cook until brown.

When the dough has risen, 'knock down' to remove the air and then add the chopped sun dried tomatoes and the fried onion and bacon, really squidging it in with the dough. When well mixed, flatten out in an oblong baking tray. Allow to prove for about ½ hour or until puffy, covering it with cling film.

Preheat the oven to 200°C/Gas mark 6/Aga equivalent.

When it has puffed up make dimple impressions with the tips of your fingers all over the dough and scatter over the sprigs of rosemary. Drizzle some extra olive oil over the top and finally sprinkle over with sea salt. Bake in a hot oven for 25-30 minutes or until the focaccia is golden brown. Turn out and cut into squares – and watch it disappear in a trice.

VARIATIONS – FOR A FILLED FOCACCIA

6 slices of Proscuitto
1 packet of feta cheese, cubed
Or 4 oz (110g) cheddar cheese, grated

This uses a mixture of sliced Proscuitto ham and feta cheese as a filling. Make the bread in the usual way. After it has proved, knock down and divide into two. Roll out one half and lay out on a baking tray in a rough rectangular shape. Add the slices of Proscuitto and scatter some cubes of feta cheese over the ham. Season with plenty of freshly ground black pepper. Roll out the remaining dough and lay on top, sealing the edges by pinching them together. Cover with cling film and allow to puff up for 30 minutes. Follow the final steps of finishing the focaccia. Eat immediately!

Somebody else can wash up!

HOMEMADE PIZZAS

If everyone helps you can at least promise them their favourite toppings. Always popular with adults and children alike.

Makes 4 individual pizzas

1½ lb (700g) strong white flour
½ pint (275ml) hot water
1 sachet easy-blend dried yeast
2 teaspoons salt
1 tablespoon olive oil

Make the dough in the usual way, this time adding olive oil instead of butter. Leave in a warm place to rise. When doubled in size, punch out the air and divide the dough into 4 sections. Roll each section into an 8 inch (20cm) circle and place on a baking tray, lightly oiled.

Pizza sauce

1 tin chopped tomatoes   Pinch dried oregano
1 onion, finely chopped   Pinch dried basil
1 clove garlic, finely chopped   1 teaspoon sugar
1 tablespoon tomato purée   Salt and pepper

While the dough is rising, prepare the sauce. The most important thing is to make a good, rich tomato sauce, which you then spread over the base of the pizza. Fry the onion in a little olive oil; add a clove of crushed garlic and a tin of ready chopped tomatoes. Add a pinch of marjoram or basil, a tablespoon of tomato purée and season well. Simmer for about ½ hour or until the sauce has reduced by half. Allow to cool before spreading over the bases.

Pizza Toppings - here are some ideas

Sliced mozzarella
   cheese
Black olives
Pepperoni
Fresh tomatoes
Sliced red onion
Flaked tuna
Red peppers, diced
Mushrooms, sliced
Anchovy fillets
Goat's cheese
Rocket
Slivers of Parmesan
Proscuitto

Preheat the oven to 220°C/Gas mark 7/ Aga equivalent.

When you have the bases ready and spread with the pizza sauce, be as creative as you like and create your own pizzas. You can scatter over chopped tomatoes and olives, crumble some goat's cheese over some rocket, but whatever you do, always finish with some mozzarella cheese on top and bake in a hot oven for about 20 minutes, or until the cheese is bubbling. Serve immediately and enjoy the results.

CHAPTER 8

Kitchen Suppers

The following recipes are old favourites and taste delicious. They have evolved over the years and we certainly never tire of having them for supper.

CHICKEN PASTA YUM

I don't know how we would have survived without this standby supper dish – it's an absolute all time Parry winner.

Serves 4

4 chicken breasts, skins removed
1 large onion, chopped
1 red pepper, de-seeded and diced
2 tins of chopped tomatoes
4 tablespoons tomato purée
A good splodge of ketchup
3-4 basil leaves
Freshly ground salt and pepper
5 fl oz (142ml carton) single cream or crème fraîche
500g packet dried pasta – either penne or shells

Heat a skillet pan and when hot, add the chicken breasts. Cook on one side for a few minutes before turning over, so that each side has chargrilled stripes. Lower the heat and allow to cook through. Once they are cooked thoroughly, remove from skillet and cut into chunks. Meanwhile, gently fry the onion in a little olive oil for a few minutes and then add the diced pepper. Add the tomatoes, tomato purée and ketchup, basil leaves and season to taste. Let it reduce to a thick tomatoey sauce and then add the chicken. Heat through. Add the single cream or crème fraîche for extra deliciousness. Cook the pasta according to the directions on the packet; drain; add cooked pasta to the tomato/chicken sauce.

SAUSAGE PASTA IN A CREAMY MUSTARD SAUCE

Serves 4

8 good quality pork sausages – skins removed. If you like spicy, go for Italian
1 onion, peeled and finely chopped
1 garlic clove, peeled and crushed
1 red pepper, de-seeded and diced
500g packet pasta (farfelle or shells are good for this recipe)
3½ fl oz (100ml carton) crème fraîche
Juice of 1 lemon
2 tablespoons of wholegrain mustard
6-8 torn basil leaves
Seasoning to taste

Fill a large pan with water and bring to the boil. Add the pasta and follow cooking instructions according to the packet. Meanwhile, fry the onion, garlic and red pepper in a little olive oil and then add the sausage meat and stir it in with the onion and pepper, until it's sizzling hot and starting to brown. Add the crème fraîche mixed in with the mustard and lemon juice, and give everything a good stir. Allow to simmer for a couple of minutes. Drain the cooked pasta and pour into the creamy sausage sauce. Season to taste and stir in the torn basil leaves. Serve with a tossed green salad.

STUFFED PANCAKES

You can use an almost limitless number of fillings for these pancakes (see below). If you use up any leftover chicken, ham or fish the trick is to make enough white sauce – use half for the filling, and the remainder for pouring over the rolled up pancakes.

Basic Pancake Mix

This quantity makes approximately 8 pancakes.

4 oz (110g) plain flour
1 egg
½ pint (275ml) milk/water mix (ratio of ¾ milk and ¼ water)
Salt and pepper

Filling options:
Ratatouille
Fresh tomato sauce
Bolognese sauce
Cooked chicken – use any left over chicken
Cooked ham
Seafood – use a mixture of prawns, crabmeat or tuna fish
½ pint (275ml) white sauce – to mix with any meat or fish

Topping:
½ pint (275ml) white sauce
6 oz (175g) mature cheddar cheese, grated

To make the pancake batter, first sift the flour into a mixing bowl, crack the egg into the middle and add the milk. Whisk fairly vigorously until you have a nice, smooth batter (the consistency of double cream). Season with salt and pepper and use when required. You can keep it in the fridge until you're ready to make the pancakes.

Preheat the oven to 180°C/Gas mark 4/Aga equivalent.

Make the pancakes in the usual way. If you use any meat or fish, mix in with the white sauce. Spoon a generous amount of filling in the centre of each pancake, roll up and place in an ovenproof dish. Pour over the remaining white sauce, sprinkle with grated cheddar cheese and bake for about 20 minutes, or until golden brown.

TOAD IN THE HOLE

(I never could work out why a toad is in the hole – I always think of a mole!)

Serves 4

8 quality pork sausages
1 red onion, finely sliced
8 rashers streaky bacon

For the batter mix:
4 oz (110g) plain flour
1 egg
½ pint (275ml) milk/water
    mix (made up of ¾ milk and ¼
    water)
Salt and pepper

Make up the pancake batter and keep in the fridge until the sausages are cooked.

Preheat the oven to 200°C/Gas mark 6/Aga equivalent.

Wrap each sausage in a rasher of streaky bacon and place in a baking dish. Scatter over the onion slices and drizzle with olive oil. Bake in a hot oven for 30-40 minutes or until the sausages are golden brown. Pour over the batter and return to the oven for a further 20 – 35 minutes, or until the batter has puffed up, golden brown with slightly crispy edges. Serve with a good onion gravy and some mashed potatoes.

SAUSAGES IN CIDER

(or 'Sausages Insider' – apologies to Cornish readers, but this must be said with strong Cornish accent!)

Serves 4

8 quality pork sausages
1 onion, sliced
2 oz (50g) butter
1 tablespoon flour
½ pint (275ml) stock (I cheat and use Marigold
    Swiss vegetable powder)
½ pint (275ml) strong, dry cider
Salt and pepper

Cook the sausages in a deep sided, cast iron griddle pan until they're starting to brown – this can take about 30-40 minutes. Remove the sausages from the pan and set aside (keep warm). Melt about 2 oz (50g) butter in the griddle pan and add the flour. Mix any remaining crusty bits of sausage in with the floury paste and gradually add the stock and cider. Return the sausages to the cider sauce and simmer for about 20 minutes, seasoning well. I serve this with a large bowl of mashed potatoes, carrots and finely shredded Savoy cabbage.

ROASTED VEGETABLE LASAGNE

The aroma of roasted vegetables wafting out of the oven is one of the reasons I like making this.

Serves 6

For the filling
2 small aubergines, diced
4 small courgettes, diced
2 lbs (900g) tomatoes, quartered
3 red peppers, de-seeded and sliced into chunks
3 yellow peppers, de-seeded and sliced into chunks
2 red onions, roughly chopped
4 cloves garlic, finely chopped
Approx 9-12 sheets of no-cook lasagne
Olive oil
Salt and pepper

Preheat the oven to 200°C/Gas mark 6/ Aga equivalent.

Prepare the vegetables and lay out on a large baking tray. Drizzle with olive oil and make sure everything is thoroughly coated with oil. Season well with salt and pepper. Roast on a high shelf in the oven for about 35 minutes or until the vegetables are just beginning to brown around the edges.

For the sauce
2 oz (50g) plain flour
2 oz (50g) butter
1 pint (570ml) milk
Few drops of Worcestershire sauce
Salt and pepper
4 oz (110g) mature Cheddar cheese, grated
10 oz (2 x 150g packs) mozzarella, drained and sliced

To make the sauce, melt the butter gently and add the flour to make a paste. Gradually add the milk, whisking to remove any lumps. Add the seasoning and stir until the sauce has thickened.

In an oblong baking dish, layer one third of the roasted vegetables, then approx 3-4 sheets lasagne, then a layer of white sauce and repeat until you have used it all up. You should finish with a layer of sauce, over which you sprinkle the cheddar cheese and mozzarella slices. Place it in a hot oven for 30-35 minutes, or until golden brown.

SPAG BOG

I make no apologies for including this very English version of an Italian ragout – it still happens to be a classic spaghetti sauce which remains faithfully popular in our family, year in, year out. I know there are many more 'proper' versions and if that's how you like to do it that's OK by me. I tend to only have beef mince (but use best quality steak mince) in the fridge or freezer so that's how I've always made mine. If I'm short on mince and need to pad it out, I include grated carrots – by the time it's cooked you'd never know there were carrots lurking, but believe, me, they add a certain sweetness to the sauce and it certainly adds bulk if you have unexpected extra guests.

Serves 4-6

1½ lb (700g) quality steak mince
2 onions, peeled and finely chopped
Olive oil
2 cloves garlic, chopped
A good shake of Worcestershire sauce
2 tins chopped tomatoes
4 carrots, peeled and grated (optional)
4 generous tablespoons tomato purée
A good squirt of tomato ketchup
1 glass red wine
Salt and freshly ground pepper
Sprinkling of dried oregano – or a handful of torn basil leaves if available
Approx 12 oz (350g) spaghetti or tagliatelle

Fry the onions with the garlic in a little olive oil. When starting to soften, add the mince and cook until the meat has gone completely brown. Add a good dash of Worcestershire sauce, the tomato purée, ketchup, a glass of red wine, dried oregano and chopped tomatoes. Add the grated carrots and season to taste. Simmer gently for about 45 minutes or until you have a nice, thick rich sauce. Serve with either spaghetti or tagliatelle, plenty of crusty French bread to mop up your plate, and a green salad. A bottle of Merlot to drink wouldn't go amiss, either.

In the mood for Italian food

SPAGHETTI ALLA CARBONARA

This is what I ate almost every day when I lived in Italy – and I still love it! This is my version, which is not truly authentic but delicious all the same.

Serves 4

9 oz (250g) streaky bacon, chopped
1 onion
2 cloves garlic, chopped
4 oz (110g) frozen peas
5 fl oz (142ml carton) single cream
2 eggs
Salt and pepper
Approx 12 oz
   (350g) spaghetti
Olive oil
Handful freshly
   grated Parmesan

Bring a large pan of water on to boil. Cook the pasta according to the directions of the packet (approx 10 minutes) – when the pasta is 'al dente', i.e. has a very slight 'bite' to it, drain in a colander and quickly rinse in hot water. Return to the pan with a little of the cooking water and cover with a lid until the bacon is cooked.

Fry the bacon in a little olive oil, add the onions and garlic and gently fry until the bacon has cooked and is starting to go brown. Throw in the peas straight from the freezer and allow to cook with the bacon (this only takes about 2 minutes to defrost). In a small bowl, pour in the cream and eggs, season well and whisk with a fork until well mixed.

Add the creamy egg mixture to the frying pan with the bacon and quickly add the drained pasta. With a wooden spoon, mix everything together and serve onto warm plates immediately. Sprinkle with some freshly grated Parmesan and serve with a green salad.

CHILLI CON CARNE

Serves 6

2 x 420g tins red kidney beans, drained and rinsed
2 x 400g tins ready chopped tomatoes
2 lb (900g) stewing steak, cut into chunks
2 onions, peeled and chopped
Dash of Worcestershire sauce
½–1 teaspoon chilli powder
1 tablespoon paprika
2 cloves garlic, peeled and chopped
3 tablespoons tomato purée
Splash of ketchup
Vegetable oil for browning the steak
2 tablespoons sour cream

Heat some oil in a casserole and when smokey hot, add the
steak, cut into 1 inch chunks, and brown both sides. Drain on
kitchen paper and set aside. In the same pan, fry the onions
and garlic in a little vegetable oil. Add the chilli powder and
paprika and continue frying for about 5 more minutes. Add
the browned meat, tomatoes, tomato purée, Worcestershire
sauce, ketchup and some salt and pepper and simmer gently
for ¾–1 hour. Add the red kidney beans 30 minutes before
the end of the cooking. Just before serving, swirl in a couple
of tablespoons of sour cream and sprinkle over with paprika.
I like to serve this with plain boiled rice or baked potatoes.

PASTA ALLA POMODORO

This is what I fall back on when there's nothing in the fridge and everyone wants supper NOW. I probably cook this more times in the year than anything else, but surprisingly no one seems to mind as it is thoroughly delicious, and what's more, it's ready in just over half an hour.

Serves 4-6

2 tins chopped tomatoes
1 large onion, peeled and finely chopped
2 cloves garlic, chopped
1 tablespoon olive oil
2 large carrots, grated
1 red pepper, de-seeded and diced
Generous squirt of tomato ketchup
2 tablespoons tomato purée
4-6 fresh tomatoes, skinned and chopped (optional extra)
Fresh basil leaves
Salt and pepper
500g packet dried penne
5 fl oz (142ml carton) single cream or crème fraîche

Fry the onion and garlic in some olive oil and add the carrots, pepper, tomatoes, ketchup and tomato purée, basil and seasoning. Add water if you think it needs a little more liquid – it does depend on how juicy the tomatoes are. Allow to simmer gently for about ½ hour. It should reduce down to a lovely, rich tomatoey sauce.

Bring a large pan of salted water on to boil. Add the pasta and cook according to directions on the packet. Drain and rinse under hot water. Return the pasta to the tomato sauce mixture and heat through. Just before serving, add the cream or crème fraîche for a touch more richness and stir in a few torn basil leaves. Serve with a crisp green salad and some French bread.

LUXURY MACARONI CHEESE

This is the real thing – full of flavour and made with a really generous amount of cheese sauce (mature Cheddar is vital). If you prefer the classic version just make the memorable cheese sauce and you will still have a damn fine macaroni cheese!

Serves 4

500g packet dried pasta – macaroni/penne/shells
1 pint (570ml) milk (if possible, full fat)
3 oz (75g) butter
3 oz (75g) plain flour
8 oz (225g) mature Cheddar cheese
1 tablespoon wholegrain mustard
6 tomatoes, sliced (optional)
9 oz (250g) streaky bacon, chopped
1 onion, chopped
1 clove garlic, chopped
Worcestershire sauce
Few drops of Tabasco
Dash of olive oil

Preheat oven to 180°C/Gas mark 4/Aga equivalent.

Put a large pan of salted water on to boil and cook the pasta according to the directions on the packet. Drain but keep lid on to retain some moisture.

In a frying pan, heat a little olive oil and fry the bacon. After a few minutes, add the chopped onion and garlic. Cook until lightly brown. Remove from the heat and set aside. To make the sauce, melt the butter in a nonstick pan, add enough flour to make a thick paste. Gradually add the milk and stir until the sauce is looking thick and creamy. Add a dash of Worcestershire sauce, plenty of freshly ground salt and pepper, a few drops of Tabasco, the mustard and add about half of the grated Cheddar cheese. Stir with a wooden spoon until the sauce is nice and creamy. Scrape all the onion and bacon into the cheese sauce and mix well.

Place the cooked pasta in a lasagne type ovenproof dish and add the sauce, mixing thoroughly. Layer over the tomatoes if you're using them, and scatter the remaining Cheddar cheese over the top. Bake for about 25-30 minutes or until the cheese is bubbling. This needs nothing more than a green salad to go with it.

SUPERIOR SHEPHERD'S PIE

This is the ultimate comfort food and is certainly delicious enough to serve as a kitchen supper dish. This version uses plenty of diced carrots and finely chopped leeks are mashed in with the spuds.

Serves 6

2lb (900g) quality steak mince
2 large onions, chopped
Dash of Worcestershire sauce
1 small jar tomato purée
Approx 4 tablespoons tomato
   ketchup
Approx 1 lb (450g) carrots,
   peeled and diced
1 small glass red wine (optional)
2 large leeks, washed and finely
   chopped
About 3lb (1.35kg) potatoes
4oz (110g) butter
Approx ½ pint (275ml) milk
Salt and pepper
4 oz (110g) grated Cheddar cheese

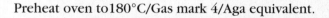

Preheat oven to180°C/Gas mark 4/Aga equivalent.

Peel the potatoes, chop each in half and place in a large saucepan of water. Add a teaspoon of salt and bring to the boil. While this is happening, put a drop of olive oil in a large casserole, add the onions and fry until they begin to golden in colour. Add the mince and cook for about 5 minutes, or until the mince has gone brown. Add the Worcestershire sauce, tomato purée and ketchup and stir in thoroughly. Some extra liquid may be added at this stage – I usually rinse out the tomato purée jar with water and add that; alternatively you could add a glass of red wine for extra richness. Add the diced carrots and simmer for about 25 minutes.

In a separate saucepan, melt a knob of butter and add the finely chopped leeks. Cook for about 5 minutes or until the leeks are nice and juicy. Leave to one side until you are ready to mash the potatoes.

When the potatoes have cooked through (after approx. ½ hour), drain and return to the saucepan. Add the butter and most of the milk and start mashing until you have a creamy mash with no lumps. Add a drop more milk if needs be and then add the leeks. Season with freshly ground salt and pepper.

Place the cooked mince in a deep oblong baking dish and add the potato/leek mash on top. Smooth over and using a fork, drag over the mash until you have made an attractive pattern. Scatter the grated cheese over the top and dot with butter.

When you are ready to eat, place in a hot oven for about 30 minutes or until golden brown. I like serving this with a finely shredded Savoy cabbage (cooked very briefly – no more than a minute or so - in a small amount of boiling water. That way the cabbage retains its glorious emerald green colour and all the vitamins!). Drain, place in a warm dish and add a knob of butter and plenty of freshly ground salt and black pepper.

Off to the shops

CHICKEN AND MUSHROOM PIE

This was brought home by our 14 year old daughter Louisa who, together with her friend Mikayla had made it from scratch, using their imagination and not a bottle of Chicken Tonight in sight!

Serves 4

8 oz (225g) ready made puff pastry
4 chicken breasts, skinned
2 large carrots, peeled and diced
1 medium tin sweetcorn, drained
½ pint (275ml) milk
1 oz (25g) butter
Tablespoon plain flour
Salt and pepper
1 teaspoon Swiss Marigold stock powder
1 lb (450g) mixture of mushrooms and leeks
   (finely sliced, cooked gently in a little
   melted butter)
1 egg, beaten

Preheat the oven to 200°C/Gas mark 6/Aga equivalent.

Chargrill the chicken in a griddle pan and when nicely browned, remove and place in a moderate oven for about 25 minutes. Place the diced carrots in a pan of water and cook until just beginning to soften. Drain, and set aside. Prepare the mushrooms and leeks and soften in a little butter.

Make the white sauce in the usual way, using plenty of seasoning and a teaspoon of stock powder. Add the cooked, diced carrots, mushrooms, leeks and the drained sweetcorn. Heat through gently for a few minutes. Remove the chicken from the oven and roughly chop; add to the sauce. Mix well and pour into a pie dish – place a ceramic bird or egg cup in the centre to allow the steam to escape. Roll out the pastry and cover over the chicken. Make leaf shapes out of any leftover pastry and brush all over with beaten egg. Cook for about 25 minutes, or until the pastry is golden brown. Serve with some mashed potato and peas for a most agreeable supper.

MUSHROOM RISOTTO

If you're lucky enough to have access to wild mushrooms, pick whatever variety you can lay your hands on. Otherwise, field mushrooms will do just fine.

Serves 4

½ oz (15g) dried porcini mushrooms
1 onion
1–2 cloves of garlic
Tablespoon olive oil
1 lb (450g) fresh mushrooms, sliced
½ oz (25g) butter
12 oz (350g) Arborio rice

1 pint (570ml) vegetable stock
4 tablespoons freshly chopped parsley
4 oz (110g) Parmesan, grated
Salt and pepper
Extra Parmesan shavings

Place the dried porcini in a bowl and cover with ¼ pint (150ml) boiling water. Leave for about 20 minutes. Drain in a sieve, reserving the liquid. Chop up the porcini and put aside.

Ideally use a heavy, cast iron saucepan for this recipe. Heat some olive oil in the pan, add the chopped onion, garlic and chopped porcini and fry for several minutes to soften. Add the rice, stirring thoroughly to ensure that it is well coated with the onions and mushrooms. Add the liquid from the porcini mushrooms and ladle most of the stock into the pan, stirring gently from time to time until the rice has absorbed all the liquid. This can take about 20 minutes. You may find that you don't need all the stock, so use your judgement.

About 5 minutes before the rice is ready, stir-fry the sliced mushrooms in a separate frying pan in a little butter until just beginning to soften. Take off the heat and return to the rice pan, stirring in the parsley and Parmesan as well. Season with salt and pepper, serve onto individual plates and grate some Parmesan shavings on top of the risotto.

CHICKEN CACCIATORE

This chicken casserole is really gutsy and full of flavour. As it's known in Italy as 'hunters' stew' it should be part of a shoot lunch repertoire!

Serves 8

8 chicken breasts, skins on
2 tablespoons plain flour
2 onions, chopped
2 cloves garlic, chopped
½ pint (275ml) red wine
½ pint (275ml) chicken stock
Basil leaves
2 tins chopped tomatoes
2 tablespoons tomato purée

4 oz (110g) de-stoned black olives, chopped
2 tablespoons parsley, chopped
Salt and pepper

Preheat the oven to 180°C/Gas mark 4/Aga equivalent.

Lightly dust the chicken pieces in flour and fry in a large pan until golden brown. Remove and place in an ovenproof dish. Add the chopped onion and garlic and cook until soft. Add the tomato purée, chopped tomatoes, wine and chicken stock and bring to the boil. Simmer gently until the sauce has reduced by half (this takes about half an hour). Season well, pour the sauce over the chicken pieces, add the chopped olives and cook in a moderate oven for about 35 minutes. Just before serving, sprinkle over with chopped parsley.

BANGERS, MASH AND RED ONION MARMALADE

When the weather is particularly cold, wet and miserable, this is what I crave! What could be more comforting than a plate full of bangers and mash, and a dollop of caramelly onion marmalade.

Serves 4

8 top quality pork sausages – choose your favourite kind
2 lb (900g) potatoes
½ pint (275ml) milk
2 oz (50g) butter

Red Onion Marmalade
1½ tablespoons groundnut or sunflower oil
4 red onions, peeled and finely sliced
3 Cox's apples, peeled, cored and cut into 8 wedges
3 teaspoons freshly grated ginger
3 tablespoons brown sugar
2 tablespoons red wine vinegar
2 tablespoons Marsala (optional)
Salt and freshly ground pepper

Start by making the onion marmalade. In a heavy based pan, heat the oil, add the onions and cook for a few minutes. Add the apples and cook for another minute or so. Tip in the remaining ingredients and bring to a simmer. Reduce the heat and cook slowly for at least a further 30 minutes, or until the onions and apples have thickened to a marmalade consistency.

Cook the sausages using whichever method you prefer – grilled, baked in the Aga or cooked in a skillet pan. Don't try and cook them too fast. Personally I think they taste better if allowed to cook gently (it can take around ¾ hour). They should be slightly crunchy round the edges in my opinion! Boil the potatoes until cooked, drain and mash thoroughly, beating in the milk and butter until you have achieved the right consistency. Season well. Serve with the onion marmalade, some good wholegrain mustard and a mixture of seasonal vegetables.

QUICK PHEASANT CURRY

This is a very easy cheat's curry if you haven't got time to make it properly.

4 pheasant breasts, skinned
1 tablespoon of vegetable oil
1oz (25g) butter
1 onion, chopped
2 garlic cloves, peeled and finely chopped
1 red pepper, diced
¼ block of creamed coconut
2 tablespoons of a good quality Balti paste
1 tin of chopped tomatoes
Salt and pepper

Heat a skillet pan, add a drop of oil and when hot, add the pheasant breasts. Char-grill for about 7 minutes each side, or until the pheasant has cooked through. Remove and cut into chunks. In another pan (cast iron Le Crueset type casserole pans are perfect for this) melt the butter and add the onion and garlic. Fry gently until softened and then add the red pepper and cook for a few minutes. Add the curry paste and coconut block and stir until the coconut has dissolved. Tip in the tomatoes, season with salt and pepper. Add the pheasant chunks and cook through for about 10 minutes. We love eating this with rice or Naan bread and a huge bowl of broccoli.

QUAIL IN RED WINE

Serves 2

4 quail, trussed
1 large onion, peeled and finely chopped
4 oz (110g) mushrooms, finely chopped
1 large clove garlic, crushed
1 dessertspoon tomato purée
½ pint (275ml) chicken stock
¼ pint (150ml) good red wine
1 bouquet garni
Salt and pepper
Tablespoon sunflower oil
Knob of butter

Preheat the oven to 180°C/Gas mark 4/Aga equivalent.

In a heavy casserole, melt a knob of butter and tablespoon of sunflower oil and when hot, brown the birds all over. Remove and set aside. Gently fry the onion, garlic and mushrooms in the same pan until soft (about 5 minutes). Return the birds to the pan and add the bouquet garni, tomato purée, stock and wine. Season to taste. Cover and cook in a moderate oven for 25-30 minutes, or until the birds are tender.

Variations:
You could substitute quail for either partridge or woodcock. You only need to roast 2 birds, and adjust the cooking times to 40-45 minutes, or until the birds are tender.

PHEASANT GOUJONS

If you have a good supply of pheasant throughout the winter, this is a brilliant way of using up the breast meat – it tastes absolutely delicious and can fool anyone into thinking it's chicken (it certainly fooled our very suspicious children when they said they didn't like pheasant!). But the secret is not to hang the pheasant for longer than 2-3 days at the very most. If the weather is mild, 2 days maximum.

Serves 4

4 pheasant breasts, cut into chunky strips
Homemade breadcrumbs, made from about ½ loaf of 2 day old white bread, baked and then blasted in a food processor until the crumbs are very fine
2 tablespoons seasoned flour
A dash of cayenne pepper
A sprinkling of paprika
2 eggs, beaten
Tablespoon sunflower oil

Heat a heavy frying pan with a tablespoon of sunflower oil. Lightly dust the strips of pheasant with seasoned flour. Dip into the beaten egg and then into the breadcrumbs, mixed in with the paprika and cayenne pepper. Fry the goujons gently until golden and crispy on the outside. Serve with chunky chips and lemon wedges.

PHEASANT IN APPLES AND CIDER

I have a weakness for strong, dry cider – so any excuse to finish the bottle…

Serves 6

6 pheasant breasts, skins removed
4 streaky bacon rashers, chopped
Seasoned flour (2 dessertspoons plain flour with a
    good sprinkling of salt and freshly ground pepper)
1 tablespoon plain flour
4 medium cooking apples, peeled and sliced
6-8 dried prunes
2 onions, peeled and chopped
2 oz (50g) butter
½ pint (275ml) strong dry cider
7 fl oz (200ml) crème fraîche
¼ pint (150ml) chicken stock
Sprig of chopped parsley

Dust the pheasant in seasoned flour. Peel and core the apples and cut into slices. Melt the butter in a heavy casserole and brown the pheasant breasts. Remove and set aside. Add the bacon rashers to the casserole pan and fry until golden. Add the onions and apples and cook for about 8 minutes. Stir in a tablespoon of flour and cook for a couple of minutes. Add the stock and cider, blend and bring to the boil. Return the pheasant breasts to the casserole and simmer (lid on) for about 15 minutes.

Just before serving, spoon in the crème fraîche and add some chopped parsley. Delicious served with some wild rice and braised red cabbage.

BARBECUE SPARE RIBS

The sauce can obviously be used with any type of meat (especially good with sausages and chicken legs). It is extremely sticky and totally delicious.

Serves 6

6 spare rib chops

Sticky Sauce:
5 tablespoons tomato ketchup
5 tablespoons apple or orange juice
3 oz (75g) dark muscavado sugar
3 tablespoons Worcestershire sauce
½ teaspoon Tabasco (more if you like it hot)
Salt and pepper

Mix all the sauce ingredients in a bowl whisk until smooth.

Lay the ribs on baking tray and cover with the sauce - use your hands to make sure the sauce has covered every inch of the meat. If you have time, marinade for ½ hour.

Preheat the oven to 200°C/Gas mark 6/Aga equivalent.

Bake for about 45 minutes to an hour, or until the meat is cooked and sauce has reduced to a really sticky glaze.

I'm not a pheasant plucker...

CLASSIC FISH PIE

I use a variety of fish – but it always includes some undyed smoked haddock as the smokey flavour really does penetrate through to give a delicious taste. If you have some salmon fillets in your freezer, they would go well too. Really, use what you like – you can add prawns or scallops too, but make sure if you're using frozen seafood to defrost thoroughly before using. Ideally use tiger prawns as they keep their shape and flavour when cooked.

Serves 8–10

1½ lb (700g) undyed smoked haddock
1 lb (450g) chunky white fish or salmon
4 oz (110g) uncooked tiger prawns (optional)
4 oz (110g) scallops (optional)
1 pint (570ml) milk
Few peppercorns
1 bay leaf
2 oz (50g) butter
2 oz (50g) plain flour
Dash of Worcestershire sauce
6 eggs, boiled and then cut in quarters
Handful of chopped parsley
4 oz (110g) grated Cheddar cheese
3 lb (1.35 kg) potatoes, peeled and quartered
Extra butter and milk for mashing potatoes

Preheat the oven to 180°C/Gas mark 4/Aga equivalent.

Place the fish in a large baking tray and cover with the milk, peppercorns and bay leaf. Simmer gently in the oven for about 20 minutes or until the fish is just beginning to flake and the skins peel off easily.

While the fish is cooking, boil the potatoes in plenty of water. Once cooked, drain and mash with plenty of butter, milk and seasoning and set aside.

Remove the fish, peel off the skin and remove any bones. Cut into rough chunks and set aside on a plate. Drain the milk into a jug as you will need this to make the white sauce.

To make the white sauce, melt the butter and add the flour to make a roux. Gradually add the left over milk from the fish, whisking gently to avoid any lumps. Add a dash of Worcestershire sauce, the parsley and the freshly ground pepper. Remove from the heat.

Arrange the fish in a large, deep and well-buttered oblong baking dish. Scatter any prawns and scallops on top and arrange the quartered eggs over the seafood. Pour the white sauce over the mixture. Add the mashed potato, smooth with a fork and scatter the grated cheddar cheese on top. Dot with butter and cook for 35-40 minutes. Garnish with parsley. I usually serve this with a large bowl of petit pois and baby carrots.

PAELLA

This classic Spanish dish is so colourful and extremely easy to make. Buy some really fresh, raw tiger prawns for the best taste.

Serves 6

Olive oil
6-8 chicken thighs
12 oz (350g) paella rice (readily available from
 supermarkets)
1 large onion, peeled and chopped
1 red pepper, de-seeded and chopped
4 oz (110g) chorizo sausage (ready sliced or buy it
 whole and dice it up).
2 cloves garlic, peeled and chopped
1 teaspoon paprika
Pinch cayenne pepper
8 oz (225g) fresh tomatoes, chopped (or 1 tin chopped
 tomatoes)
1 pint (570ml) chicken stock
12 large raw tiger prawns (keep some whole for
 decoration; remove heads on the rest)
2 oz (50g) frozen peas
1 large lemon, cut into wedges
Salt and pepper

If you haven't got a paella pan (and I haven't), use your largest, widest frying pan and it does the job just as well.

Heat some olive oil and when hot, add the chicken thighs. Fry until golden brown, remove from the pan and keep warm in a moderate oven for the next 10 minutes or so.

Gently fry the onion, garlic, pepper and chorizo in the same pan until beginning to go brown. Add the paprika and cayenne pepper, followed by the rice, stirring it into the onion and pepper mixture. Add the tomatoes and chicken stock and bring to the boil and simmer gently for about 10 minutes.

Return the chicken to the pan, add the frozen peas and raw prawns and continue simmering for a further 15-20 minutes. A touch more liquid may be needed to prevent the rice sticking to the pan.

The prawns will magically turn pink while they cook and the chicken will have cooked through by this time. Season with salt and pepper. Garnish with lemon wedges and serve immediately.

SUNDAY LUNCH

Roast Beef and Yorkshire Pudding – cooked by Pickle, carved by Mango

Rub rib of beef with mustard, surround with a quartered onion. Put into hot oven for 1½ hours.

Prepare the veg.

Mix batter for Yorkshire Puddings.

Remove beef and allow to relax.

Use juices to make gravy.

Pour batter in Yorkshire Pudding tin.

Present perfect puddings and ... CARVE!

CHAPTER 9

Divine Dinners
or slightly more grown-up entertaining

Once in a while you
know you've got to get out of the kitchen and into the dining room. You may decide
to go the whole hog and do a buffet party for 30 – whatever the reason, you may
need to cook something a little more special.

RARE FILLET OF BEEF

We cooked this for our daughter's 18th birthday party and were so amazed at how easy it was – and how rewarding the comments were! It's ideal to make as part of a buffet lunch or dinner for around 20 people, so I am assuming you will be serving other dishes.

6 lb (approx 2.7 kg) fillet beef
Olive oil
3-4 tablespoons crushed peppercorns
Salt
Watercress – to decorate

Preheat the oven to 230°C/Gas mark 8/ Aga equivalent.

Crush the peppercorns in a pestle and mortar and lay them out on a large baking tray. Rub the beef with a little olive oil and roll it over the peppercorns. Season with salt and place in a very hot oven for exactly 30 minutes if you like your beef pink in the middle. Leave to cool and then wrap in foil and refrigerate until ready to use. Cut the beef into thin slices and arrange on a large platter. Decorate with watercress. Serve with a creamy horseradish sauce.

LAMB SHREWSBURY

The redcurrant jelly is the secret to this recipe – the sauce is beautifully rich and transforms the lamb into a truly memorable meal. As an alternative to using lamb chops, you could roast a lamb in the usual way and serve the sauce separately.

Serves 4

8 lamb cutlets (dusted in a little seasoned flour)
1 onion
1 tablespoon plain flour
1 teaspoon mustard powder
1 jar good quality redcurrant jelly

3 tablespoons Worcestershire sauce
¼ pint (150ml) red wine
Juice 1 lemon
Salt and pepper
Tablespoon olive oil
Knob of butter

Preheat the oven to 170°C/Gas mark 3/Aga equivalent.

Lightly oil a heavy frying pan and when hot, sear the chops for a few minutes on each side until starting to brown in colour. Remove and keep warm. In the same pan, melt a knob of butter, add the flour and mustard to the juices of the chops and mix together to form a paste. Gradually add the wine, mixing well with a wooden spoon. Finally add the redcurrant jelly, Worcestershire sauce, lemon juice and seasoning. Mix well to make a smooth glossy sauce. Place the cutlets in an ovenproof dish, pour over the redcurrant sauce and return to a moderate oven for about 30 minutes. I like to serve this with some oven roasted diced potatoes, carrots and green beans for a delicious supper.

MINI BEEF WELLINGTONS

If you want to impress guests then this is the one to do. You can prepare it in advance and it takes hardly any time to cook.

Serves 8

8 x 6 oz (175g) fillet steaks –
   choose nice thick slices from the
   middle of the fillet
425g pack of ready made puff pastry
   (gives you 2 sheets)
2 eggs, beaten
½ pint (275ml) red wine
Bunch of watercress for decoration

For the filling:
1 lb (450g) field
   mushrooms
2 large onions
2 oz butter
salt and pepper

Blitz the onions in a food processor until very finely chopped. Remove and replace with the mushrooms and repeat the process. In a medium saucepan, melt the butter and add the onion and mushroom mix. Cook very slowly until all the mushroom juices have evaporated and you are left with what looks like a paste. Place in a bowl and allow to cool; cover with cling-film and refrigerate.

Prepare the beef a few hours before serving by heating a frying pan with a little oil and when it's smoky hot, add the steaks and cook for ½ minute each side, so that they are sealed. Remove and allow to cool. Deglaze the frying pan with the red wine and two tablespoons of the mushroom mixture. Boil until the sauce has reduced by a third. Set aside. Roll out the pastry – you want it fairly thin - and cut into 8 equal pieces, about 8 inches (20 cm) square. Reserve any trimmings for decoration. Season each steak with salt and

pepper and place a piece of steak onto each square of pastry. Place about a tablespoon of the mushroom mixture on top of the steak. Bring together each diagonal corner of the pastry square and pinch together. Repeat with the other side and overlap if necessary.

Don't seal the pastry too tightly, as it needs room to expand when cooking. Brush with beaten egg and decorate with pastry leaves if you want. Place the steaks on a greased baking tray and chill until ready to cook.

Preheat the oven to 220°C/Gas mark 7/Aga equivalent.

Place the tray on a high shelf in the oven for about 25 minutes if you like your steak medium rare (i.e. pink in the middle). Allow a further 5 minutes for medium or 5 minutes less for rare. Warm the sauce and drizzle it around each parcel. Garnish with watercress and serve immediately to prevent the steaks from over-cooking.

BONED LEG OF LAMB WITH APRICOT, PRUNE AND ROSEMARY STUFFING

My eldest daughter Sophie knows how to bone a lamb, but since I don't I ask my butcher to do the job for me. Buy a medium size leg of lamb, trimmed of excess fat.

Serves 6

1 leg of lamb, boned

Stuffing:
3 oz (75g) apricots (ready to eat)
3 oz (75g) prunes (ready to eat)
2 shallots, finely chopped
8 oz (225g) fresh white breadcrumbs
Leaves from a sprig of rosemary, finely chopped
Juice and zest of an orange (half for the stuffing, half for the
   sauce)
Salt and pepper
Cranberry sauce (1 small jar)
3 tablespoons Grand Marnier (optional)
Extra rosemary leaves

Chop up the apricots and prunes and place in a bowl with the shallots, rosemary leaves and breadcrumbs. Mix in half the orange juice and zest and season with salt and pepper.

Preheat the oven to 200°C/Gas mark 6/Aga equivalent.

Stuff the leg of lamb and pin the end flaps over with skewers. Tie the meat firmly with string so that it resembles a roll. Cover the top of the lamb roll with cranberry sauce and sprinkle with fresh rosemary leaves. Place in a roasting tin and roast for about 1 hour. Remove the meat from the tin. Cover with foil and keep warm for about 20 minutes.

Pour off the fat from the roasting tin and deglaze with Grand Marnier and the remaining orange juice. Simmer for 5 minutes, stirring well to ensure that all the crunchy bits are included in the sauce. Pour the sauce through a sieve into a jug and keep warm. When ready to serve, place the stuffed lamb on a large serving platter and garnish with a few rosemary leaves. I like to serve this with aubergine and tomato slices.

BEEF PUTTANESCA

This is a heart-warming dish for a cold winter's day – the olives and chilli flakes give the stew a real kick. Delicious served with piping hot baked potatoes.

Serves 4

Approx 8 oz (225g) beef stewing steak, diced
2 red peppers, de-seeded
2 yellow peppers, de-seeded
2 cloves garlic, chopped
1 onion, peeled and chopped
2 tins chopped tomatoes
2 tablespoons tomato purée
1 teaspoon paprika
Small can pitted black olives, drained
Just a pinch of dried chilli flakes
Salt and pepper
Olive oil
Sour cream (optional)

Preheat oven to 180°C/Gas mark 4/Aga equivalent.

Cut each pepper into 4 slices; place in a baking tray and add the chopped garlic. Drizzle with olive oil and roast in a hot oven until just beginning to brown around the edges. Remove from oven. Heat a little olive oil in a casserole dish and brown the diced beef in batches. Add the roasted peppers and the rest of the ingredients and stir thoroughly. Season to taste. Cook in a moderate oven for about 45 minutes or until the beef is tender. You could swirl a tablespoon of sour cream into the beef just before serving, sprinkled with a little extra paprika.

PORK AND PROSCUITTO PARCELS

This is the ideal recipe if you want to offer something a bit more special… But I promise it's incredibly easy to make and it seems to impress anyone who's ever eaten it.

Serves 6

2 chunky lengths of pork
    tenderloin, weighing about
    2lb (900g)   Juice of 1 lemon
12 slices of Proscuitto   Salt and pepper
12 sage leaves   Olive oil
200g crème fraîche   Butter

Cut the pork into 1 inch (2.5cm) chunks and flatten with a mallet. Season with salt and pepper. Lay each flattened pork over a slice of proscuitto and add a sage leaf on top. Roll up, securing with a cocktail stick. You need approximately two 'rolls' per person.

Heat a small knob of butter and a tablespoon of olive oil in a wide frying pan and when hot, add the pork rolls. Fry for a few minutes on one side and then turn over until cooked through and both sides are brown (the smell at this stage is mouth watering). Remove from the pan and place on a serving dish – keep warm. Add the crème fraîche to the juices of the frying pan; add a squeeze of lemon and season with black pepper. Remove the cocktail sticks from each 'roll' and pour over the creamy sauce. I tend to serve this on a bed of wilted spinach.

PHEASANT UNDER THE EIDERDOWN

If you have a glut of pheasants you can afford to be generous, and I would suggest you roast 2 pheasants to serve 4 people.

2 pheasants
6 rashers of streaky bacon
12 juniper berries
2 oz (50g) butter
1 level dessertspoon plain flour
½ pint (275ml) chicken stock
200g crème fraîche or the equivalent of yoghurt and cream
   combined
1 dessertspoon of cranberry sauce
Juice of one lemon
Salt and pepper

Preheat the oven to 180°C/Gas mark 4/Aga equivalent.

Smother the pheasants with butter and arrange the rashers of bacon over each bird. Season with salt and pepper. Tuck the juniper berries into each pheasant cavity and place in a roasting tin. Roast for about 45 minutes to 1 hour or until their juices run clear. When cooked, remove from the pan and place on a plate. Cover in foil and leave in a warm place for 10 minutes. Reserve the crispy bacon slices for later use.

Heat the juices of the birds (left in the roasting tin) and add the flour; blend together and slowly add the stock. Add the lemon juice and cranberry sauce, allow to reduce and thicken. Take off the heat and add the crème fraîche or yoghurt/cream mix. Place over a low heat until well blended (do not boil or the mixture could curdle). Remove from the heat and keep warm.

To serve, joint the pheasants into 8 pieces and arrange on a shallow platter. Pour over the sauce and scatter over some of the reserved crispy bacon (roughly chopped).

CHAPTER 10

Perfect Puds

Puddings…the very word conjures up all kinds of delight and those who know me well know how much I love them! If it's a choice between a starter and pudding then the pudding will win. I especially love the traditional English puddings – crumbles, steamed puddings and tarts. Puddings for me come into their own in the winter months, when somehow I can justify having a bowl of sticky toffee pudding with lashings of custard and feel I can get away with it. The summer months offer up entirely different desires, when you can't beat a delicious summer pudding made with fresh summer fruits on a hot summer's day.

STICKY TOFFEE PUDDING

When this first appeared on pub menus I could not imagine a more delectable offering. This version works well for me, and in our family is a substitute for Christmas pudding. I make it in a 9 inch (23cm) sandwich tin and it feeds about 12 people easily.

4 oz (110g) butter
6 oz (175g) caster sugar
3 eggs, beaten
8 oz (225g) self raising flour, sifted
8 oz (225g) stoned dates
8 fl oz (225ml) boiling water
1 teaspoon pure vanilla extract
1 teaspoon bicarbonate of soda
2 oz (50g) chopped walnuts

Preheat the oven to 180°C/Gas mark 4/Aga equivalent.

Put the dates in a bowl and add the boiling water to soften them. Add the vanilla extract, bicarbonate of soda and leave to cool.

Cream together the butter and sugar until the mixture is light and creamy. Add the beaten eggs in small amounts and beat them into the mixture. Fold in the sifted flour using a metal spoon and then fold in the cooled mixture of chopped dates and water.
Add the walnuts and fold once more. Don't panic if the mixture looks too sloppy – it's meant to! Pour the mixture into a lightly greased 9 inch (23cm) sandwich tin and bake for about 25 -30 minutes. When the cake has cooled slightly, turn onto a large plate and pour the toffee sauce over it. Serve warm with plenty of cream. Indulge yourself.

Toffee Sauce
This is the best bit and to hell with the calories
8 oz (225g) soft brown sugar
6 oz (175g) butter
8 tablespoons double cream

This is very easy – all that is required is for everything to go into a saucepan and heat gently until the sugar has dissolved and the butter has melted.

Baby sitting

BLACKBERRY AND APPLE CRUMBLE

Blackberry picking is fun, if a little prickly, and you end up with very purple hands. Mango the Labrador adores blackberries and doesn't seem to mind that the walk has frequent interruptions. It is most rewarding coming home with a large basket of free produce, and best of all, you get to eat a classic pudding.

Serves 6

4 large cooking apples, peeled, cored and sliced
Approx. 8 oz (225g) blackberries, washed in a sieve under
   running water and any grubs removed!
   Or 1 bag of frozen summer fruits
   (does not have to be defrosted first)
4 oz (110g) caster sugar

Crumble topping
We love lots of crumble (to be honest, the crumble is the best bit). So I make no secret of the fact that this is really double what you need, but what the heck.

10 oz (275g) plain flour
5 oz (150g) butter
5 oz (150g) caster sugar
Large tablespoon demerara sugar

Preheat the oven to 180°C/Gas mark 4/Aga equivalent. Place the sliced apples and blackberries (or the frozen summer fruits) in a saucepan, add the sugar and allow to simmer gently until the apples are soft and the blackberries are oozing juice. Remove and arrange in an oblong baking dish. Allow to cool a little before adding the crumble topping.

Mix together the flour and butter until the mixture resembles breadcrumbs. Add the sugar, and with your hands, really mix it together – I find that the heat from my hands makes the crumble look nice and knobbly. Sprinkle this over the cooled fruit and add a sprinkling of demerara sugar for extra crunch. Bake for about half an hour, or until the crumble is just going golden brown. Serve with plenty of thick warm custard and a jug of fresh cream.

RASPBERRY AND APPLE COCONUT CRUMBLE

I love the combination of raspberries and apples, and the coconut makes a delicious tasting crumble.

Serves 6

4 Granny Smith apples, peeled, cored and thinly sliced
Juice of 1 lemon
2 punnets of raspberries
6 oz (175g) plain flour
6 oz (175g) desiccated coconut
6 oz (175g) soft brown sugar
Sprinkling of freshly grated nutmeg
8 oz (225g) unsalted butter

Preheat the oven to 190°C/Gas mark 5/Aga equivalent.

Arrange the apple slices in a buttered, shallow oven dish. Sprinkle with lemon juice to prevent them discolouring. Spread over the raspberries. Mix the flour, coconut, sugar, nutmeg and butter in a food processor and whizz until crumbly. Cover the fruit with the crumble topping and gently pat down so that the top is smooth. Bake for 30 minutes or until the topping is golden brown. Serve with some fresh cream or crème fraîche.

EVE'S PUDDING

This is even more delicious eaten cold from the fridge the next day (assuming there are any leftovers!).

Serves 6

4 large cooking apples, peeled, cored and sliced
4 oz (110g) caster sugar
8 oz (225g) butter, softened
8 oz (225g) soft brown sugar
8 oz (225g) ground almonds
4 eggs, beaten
1 packet of flaked almonds

Preheat the oven to 180°C/Gas mark 4/Aga equivalent.

Place the apples and caster sugar in a pan and simmer gently until the apples are soft and oozing juice. Remove and place in an oblong baking dish.

Mix the softened butter and sugar until smooth and creamy. Beat in the eggs a little at a time, and then fold in the ground almonds. Spread the mixture over the fruit, but don't worry if it doesn't cover the fruit completely – by the time it's cooked it will have magically spread out! Sprinkle over the flaked almonds and bake for about 45 minutes, or until golden. Delicious served with vanilla ice cream.

BREAD AND BUTTER PUDDING

This classic English pudding is so good and I'm glad to see it making a comeback. I've also included a couple of good variations.

Serves 6

6 slices of white bread from a good quality loaf, crusts left on
2 oz (50g) butter
4 oz (110g) plump sultanas
2 oz (50g) raisins
3 eggs
2 oz (50g) caster sugar
1 pint milk (570ml) (or a mixture of milk and double cream for a more
   luxurious custard)
Zest of 1 lemon
2 tablespoons demerara sugar

Preheat the oven to 180°C/Gas mark 4/Aga equivalent.

Butter the bread and cut into triangles. Line a buttered oblong pie dish with the triangles and scatter the sultanas and raisins over the top. Whisk the milk, eggs, sugar and lemon zest in a small bowl and strain over the bread and fruit. Leave to soak for about ½ hour (it can be left overnight in the fridge). Before baking, sprinkle some demerara sugar over the top, and dot with butter. Bake for about 30-40 minutes or until golden brown.

Variations:
Cut slices of Italian pannetone cake, spread with butter and add the custard topping. Bake as above.

Slice 6 croissants in half (no butter needed) and pour over ¼ tin of warmed golden syrup. Add the custard and bake as above.

GOOSEBERRY AND ELDERFLOWER FOOL

Fruit fools are delicious summer puddings, and if you make your own elderflower cordial it adds a special flavour to the gooseberries.

Serves 4-6

1½ lb (700g) gooseberries
2 tablespoons water
8 fl oz (220ml) elderflower
   cordial
Caster sugar (to taste)
1 pint (570ml) double cream

Simmer the gooseberries in the water until they are soft. Either whizz in a food processor (you may still have to press through a sieve to achieve a velvety smoothness). Add the cordial to the purée, and sweeten with sugar to taste. Whip the cream and fold into the purée. Transfer to a serving bowl, cover with cling-film and chill for several hours.

STEAMED TREACLE PUDDING

This is the ultimate winter comfort pudding and I just love it!

Serves 4

4 oz (110g) butter, softened
4 oz (110g) caster sugar
6 oz (175g) self-raising flour, sifted
Pinch of salt

2 large eggs, beaten
Few drops pure vanilla extract
2-3 tablespoons milk
2 tablespoons golden syrup

Use a large steamer or saucepan and half fill it with water. Bring to the boil. Lightly butter a 1½ pint pudding basin and pour the syrup into the bowl.

Cream together the butter and sugar until light and creamy. Stir in the vanilla extract and add the eggs, a little at a time. Fold in the sifted flour and salt, and add enough milk to give it a dropping consistency. Spoon the mixture into the prepared bowl.

Cover with a piece of double-thick greaseproof paper or foil, and secure with string. Lower the bowl into the boiling water and ensure that the water comes no more than two thirds of the way up the side of the bowl. Steam for 1½ hours (if necessary, top up the pan with boiling water). Do not allow to boil dry! When the pudding is ready, run a knife around the inside of the bowl to loosen the pudding.

Turn out onto a warm plate and serve with lashings of custard.

Variations: sprinkle a few currants, raisins and sultanas into the bottom of the bowl and stir 2 oz (50g) of the mixed fruit into the pudding.

BANOFFI PIE

A little goes a long way with this highly calorific pudding!

Serves 6–8

2 x 397g tins condensed milk
8 oz (225g) digestive biscuits
4 oz (110g) butter
4 bananas, peeled and sliced
5 fl oz (142ml carton) whipping cream

Place the tins of unopened condensed milk in a large pan, fill with enough water to cover the tins and bring to the boil. Continue boiling for 4 hours, and whatever you do, don't allow it to boil dry (as happened to me once…very messy!). Cool slightly before opening the lids – you will be rewarded with a lovely toffee sauce.

Blitz the digestives in a food processor for several seconds. Melt the butter in a pan, add the digestives and stir well. Place in an 8 inch (20cm) spring-form tin, using the back of a spoon to smooth down the mixture. Chill for several hours in the fridge.

Just before serving, pour the toffee sauce over the biscuit base and smooth over with a spoon. Add slices of chopped banana over the toffee. Whip the cream and either pipe or spread this over the bananas. Decorate with a few extra banana slices.

CHOCOLATE POTS

One of the simplest, yet most delicious, puddings I know. Make sure you use a good quality chocolate (minimum 70% cocoa solids). The quantities are always 1 egg and 2 oz (50g) chocolate per person, so it's easy to work out whatever the number of people.

Serves 6

6 large eggs
12 oz (350g) quality dark chocolate
Zest of 1 orange

Break up the chocolate into a small bowl and melt gently by placing the bowl over a saucepan of simmering water.

You need one large mixing bowl and one small one. Crack the egg whites into the large bowl and the yolks into the small bowl. Add the melted chocolate to the egg yolks, and beat well until smooth and glossy. Stir in the orange zest.

Whisk the egg whites until stiff peaks have formed. With a metal spoon, carefully fold a spoonful of the chocolate mixture into the egg whites. Continue until all the chocolate is incorporated into the whites. Spoon into ramekins or small espresso cups. Chill in the fridge for at least an hour before serving.

CHOCOLATE ICE BOX CAKE

This is, in fact, a pudding – not just any old pudding, either, but my mother's recipe which she was given in Beirut in 1953 by one of her Canadian friends. This is the ultimate, perfect party pudding.

Serves 8

8 oz (225g) plain chocolate (minimum 70% cocoa solids)
24 sponge fingers
8 large eggs, separated
10 fl oz (284ml carton) double cream – or use half cream/half crème fraîche if you prefer
Drop of brandy, rum or whisky (optional)

For decoration:
A little whipped cream – Chocolate shavings

Melt the chocolate in a bowl over simmering (not boiling) water. Take off the heat and cool slightly. Add the egg yolks one at a time into the melted chocolate, beating well in between. Whisk the egg whites until stiff and fold the chocolate mixture into the whites, incorporating as much air as possible. You could add some alcohol at this stage, about a tablespoon of either brandy, rum or whisky. Whip the cream (or a mixture of double cream and crème fraîche, in which case just fold the crème fraîche into the whipped cream) and fold into the mousse.

Place a layer of sponge fingers on the bottom of a deep glass bowl. Pour over some of the mousse mixture, and continue layering until you have the chocolate mousse on top. Decorate with some extra whipped cream and chocolate shavings. Chill in the fridge before serving.

Time for a chat

CHOCOLATE AND RASPBERRY ROULADE

This never fails to impress, and although it almost always cracks when you fold it, a light dusting of icing sugar makes it look like it's meant to crack! I think raspberries and chocolate make very good partners, which is why I like this version of such a classic pudding so much.

Serves 8-10

For the roulade
6 oz (175g) good quality chocolate (minimum 70% cocoa
   solids) – plus a little extra for decoration
6 eggs, separated
6 oz (175g) caster sugar
Icing sugar for decoration

For the filling
10 fl oz (284ml carton) double cream
1 lb (450g) fresh raspberries
1 tablespoon caster sugar

Preheat the oven to 180°C/Gas mark 4/Aga equivalent.

First line a Swiss roll tin about 8 x 10 inches (20 x 25 cm) with a sheet of parchment paper.

Melt the chocolate in a bowl over a saucepan of gently simmering water. Whisk the egg yolks in a mixing bowl and gradually add the caster sugar, whisking until the mixture is thick and creamy. Stir in the melted chocolate and mix well. In a large, spotlessly clean mixing bowl whisk the egg whites until stiff. Using a metal spoon, fold the chocolate mixture into the stiffened egg whites. Pour into the prepared tin and bake in a moderate oven for about 15 minutes, or until firm to touch. Remove from the oven, cover with a damp teatowel and allow to cool.

The next bit sounds fiddly but isn't as bad as it sounds. Place a new piece of parchment paper on your working surface and lightly dust with icing sugar. Uncover the roulade and flip it onto the prepared paper. Peel off the paper sticking to the roulade. Whip the cream and spread it over the roulade. Spoon over the raspberries, and sprinkle over the caster sugar. Roll the roulade up lengthways (this is when it inevitably cracks) and slip it onto a serving platter. Just before serving, sieve the icing sugar over the roulade and shave a little extra chocolate over the top.

SUMMER PUDDING

This is so popular that it was even requested as a Christmas Day pudding! The only thing to remember is to make it the night before, to allow all the juices of the fruits to soak into the bread.

Serves 6

1½ lb (about 700g) mixed summer fruits – can be a combination of strawberries, raspberries, redcurrants or blackberries
4 oz (110g) caster sugar
Half a loaf of day old sliced white bread, crusts removed

Place the fruits in a pan, add the sugar and simmer gently for about 5 minutes or until the juices are running and the fruit is soft.

Line the inside of a 1½ pint pudding basin with slices of white bread (cut into triangles), making sure there are no gaps. Keep a few slices reserved to place on top of the bowl.

Ladle the fruit into the bread-lined basin, reserving about 4 tablespoons of the juice, which you need later. Sit the bowl on a plate (to catch any juice), cover with the remaining bread and place a heavy weight (or about 8 small plates) to weight it down, and place in the fridge overnight.

When you're ready to eat, place a serving plate over the top, flip the bowl and plate over and it should come out of the basin easily. Use the reserved fruit juice to pour over any 'white' areas. Serve with a jug of chilled cream.

BROWN BREAD ICE CREAM

This may sound a bit strange, but what you have is effectively a praline made with breadcrumbs and sugar and it tastes superb.

Serves 6

3 oz (75g) fresh wholemeal breadcrumbs
2 oz (50g) demerara sugar
4 eggs, separated
4 oz (110g) caster sugar
10 fl oz (284ml carton) double cream

Put some foil on baking sheets and sprinkle the breadcrumbs and demerara sugar over it. Either grill or bake in a hot oven for about 5 minutes, turning the crumbs over half way through. When the bread and sugar have caramelised remove and leave to get completely cold.

Whisk the egg yolks in a small bowl until well beaten. Whisk the egg whites in a large mixing bowl until stiff, finally adding the caster sugar in small amounts. Whip the cream and fold into the meringue mixture and then add the beaten egg yolks and the breadcrumb mix. Mix well and pour into an empty ice cream carton or plastic box and freeze for at least two hours.

Take the ice cream out of the freezer about 5 minutes before you serve.

PAVLOVA

What a glorious concoction this pudding is – piled high with whipped cream and spilling over with fresh fruit, it is quite sensational.

Serves 8

4 egg whites
8 oz (225g) caster sugar
2 teaspoons cornflower
1 teaspoon white wine vinegar
½ teaspoon pure vanilla extract

Filling:
10 fl oz (284ml carton) whipping cream
Fresh summer fruits – strawberries, raspberries, redcurrants, blackberries
Or tropical fruits – passion fruit, bananas, pineapples, kiwi fruit

Line a baking tray with a 9 inch (23 cm) circular sheet of parchment paper.

Preheat the oven to 140°C/Gas mark 1/Aga equivalent.

Whisk the egg whites using an electric whisk until stiff. Add the sugar, a tablespoon at a time, and whisk into the egg whites until glossy. Fold in the cornflour, white wine vinegar and vanilla extract. Swirl the meringue mixture over the parchment paper making a slight hollow in the centre.

Bake for about 1¼ hours or until firm to touch. Allow to cool before removing the parchment paper. Transfer to a large plate and spread the whipped cream over the base. Fill with any fresh, seasonal fruit – you could go for tropical fruits or traditional summer fruits, both are delicious. Dust with a little icing sugar before serving.

MERINGUES

Always a favourite. The trick is getting them crisp on the outside and unbelievably chewy in the middle. The ratio is always 1 egg white to 2 oz (50g) caster sugar.

This makes approx 16 meringues

4 egg whites
8oz (225g) caster sugar

Preheat oven to 140C/Gas mark 1/ Aga equivalent.

Before you start, do make sure the mixing bowl is spotlessly clean and free from grease. Whisk the egg whites using an electric whisk to do the legwork. When you've reached the 'soft peak' stage, add the sugar a tablespoon at a time and whisk into the whites. Line 2 baking trays with non-stick paper and place heaped tablespoons of the meringue in rows, allowing a bit of a gap between each one. Bake in a very moderate oven for about an hour (ovens vary so much you'll have to keep checking).

BLACKBERRY CRUMBLE ICE CREAM

If you have an ice cream maker this would be a doddle to make. Sadly I don't, but it only takes a bit more effort, and believe me, the result is worth that effort as it is a sensational ice cream.

Serves 6

About 1 lb (500g) blackberries (or a mixed bag of frozen
    summer fruits if there aren't any blackberries)
3 tablespoons caster sugar
10 fl oz (284ml carton) double cream
500g carton fresh custard
1 teaspoon pure vanilla extract

For the crumble:
2 oz (50g) crunchy oat cereal, or 2 oz (50g) porridge oats,
or 2 oz (50g) crushed Amaretti biscuits
2 oz (50g) butter, melted
2 oz (50g) demerara sugar

Place the blackberries (or frozen summer fruits) in a pan, add the sugar and gently simmer for about 5 minutes (a little longer if using frozen fruits), or until the juices start to run and the fruit has softened. Place in a food processor and whizz for a second to purée the fruit. If you like your purée very smooth, pass through a sieve for a velvety smooth texture. Chill in a bowl until ready to use.

Whip the cream in a large bowl until just beginning to hold its shape, add the carton of custard and the vanilla extract. If you have an ice cream maker, place the mixture into the machine and process until softly set. Alternatively, place the mixture in a plastic container and freeze for about 2 hours, or until the outer edge is set. Remove from the freezer, gently whisk to remove any crystals, and return to the freezer for a further 1-2 hours, or until softly set.

Preheat the oven to 180°C/Gas mark 4/Aga equivalent.

Place all the crumble ingredients in a bowl and mix thoroughly. Spread onto a greased baking tray lined with non-stick paper and cook for about 5 - 10 minutes, or until starting to brown. When cool enough to handle, break into pieces and leave to cool.

When the ice cream is ready, sprinkle over half the crumble and half the purée and gently fold into the ice cream, making a swirling pattern as you do so. Return to the freezer until firm. 30 minutes before serving, remove from the freezer and allow to 'relax'. Serve in glass bowls with a little of the remaining sauce and crumble topping sprinkled over the top. It will keep for about a month

TOBLERONE CREAM

Our eldest daughter Sophie spent four months as a chalet girl in France, and this was a favourite with her guests. It has to be one of the quickest, easiest puddings ever.

Serves 8–10

1 large Toblerone bar
1 pint (570ml) double cream

Melt the Toblerone in a bowl over a pan of gently simmering water. Allow to cool slightly.
Whip the cream in a mixing bowl until fairly stiff and add the melted chocolate. Pour into a plastic container and either freeze and eat as ice cream, or pour into ramekins, chill and serve as a sort of mousse.

Either way it is divine.

EASY STRAWBERRY ICE CREAM

The beauty of this ice cream is that it requires no machines or endless beatings, so is dead easy to make. It also works well with raspberries or blackberries.

Serves 6

1 lb (450g) fresh strawberries (or raspberries)
8 oz (225g) icing sugar, sifted
10 fl oz (284ml carton) double cream, lightly whipped

Mash or liquidise the strawberries. Rub through a sieve to remove any seeds (especially if you use raspberries instead). Slowly stir in the icing sugar and then fold in the whipped cream. Pour into a plastic container and freeze for at least 4-5 hours.

Party time

CHAPTER 11

Tempting Tarts & Pies

Making tarts is without doubt one of the most therapeutic culinary tasks I can think of. Just making the pastry calms me, and when you produce the tart in all its glory it's an extremely satisfying feeling. Here is a selection of my personal favourites.

I use two types of pastry for the tarts, shortcrust and pâte sucrée. I've listed the ingredients for both, and thereafter just refer to which type to use.

Shortcrust Pastry
8 oz (225g) plain flour
Pinch salt
2 oz (50g) butter
2 oz (50g) lard
Approx. 4-5 tablespoons water

Sift the flour and salt into a bowl. Using your fingertips, cut up the fat and rub into the flour until it resembles fine breadcrumbs. Add the water a tablespoon at a time and use a knife to bind it together to form a ball, leaving the sides of the bowl clean. Wrap in cling-film and refrigerate for an hour.

Pâte Sucrée
8 oz (225g) plain flour
Pinch salt
4 oz (110g) butter
2 oz (50g) icing sugar
2 egg yolks

Sift the flour and salt into a bowl. Add the butter and work into the flour until it resembles fine breadcrumbs. Add the sifted icing sugar and egg yolks and blend until all the flour comes away from the edge of the bowl and the mixture binds into a ball. Wrap in cling-film and refrigerate for an hour.

BAKEWELL TART

The combination of raspberry jam and the fragrant almond filling makes this one of my top 10 tarts. I use a 10 inch (25cm) metal fluted tart tin.

8 oz (225g) shortcrust pastry

For the filling:
Raspberry jam
4 oz (110g) unsalted butter
4 oz (110g) caster sugar
3 oz (75g) ground almonds
2 eggs, beaten
1 small packet of flaked almonds

Preheat the oven to 200°C/gas mark 6/Aga equivalent.

Melt the butter gently in a saucepan and add the sugar, stirring together. Take the pan off the heat and add the beaten eggs and ground almonds and mix thoroughly.

Make the pastry in the usual way, and chill for an hour. When ready to use, roll out the pastry and line the fluted tin. Prick the pastry base with a fork and spread the jam thickly over the base. Pour over the almond mix and sprinkle the flaked almonds over the top. Bake in a hot oven for about 30 minutes.

LEMON MERINGUE PIE

8 oz (225g) pâte sucrée

Lemon Filling
Grated zest and juice of 3 lemons
2 oz (50g) cornflour
½ pint (275ml) water
4 oz (110g) caster sugar
3 large egg yolks
Beaten egg for glazing

Meringue
3 large egg whites
6 oz (175g) caster sugar

Preheat the oven to 200°C/Gas mark 6/Aga equivalent.

Roll out the chilled pastry and line a 10 inch (25 cm) metal fluted flan tin. Prick the base of the pastry and cook in a hot oven for about 15 minutes. Remove from the oven and brush the inside with a little beaten egg yolk; return to finish cooking for about 5-10 minutes or until the pastry is golden in colour.

Place the cornflour in a small bowl and add 2 tablespoons water; blend to make a paste. In a saucepan, add the sugar, zest of 3 lemons, the cornflour paste and the remaining water. Whisk over a gentle heat until everything has mixed together, and then increase the heat until the mixture has thickened. Cook for about a minute, then remove from the heat. Stir in the lemon juice and egg yolks and mix well. Cool slightly before pouring into the pastry case.

Lower the oven temperature to 150°C/Gas mark 2/Aga equivalent.

Whisk the egg whites until stiff, add half the sugar and whisk again until stiff. Fold in the remaining sugar and when mixed in, spread over the lemon filling. Bake for 20-30 minutes or until the meringue tips are golden.

APPLE AND AMARETTI TART

Each Christmas we receive a wonderful box of Italian delicacies, including Amaretti biscuits – this is one way of enjoying them.

Serves 6

For the base
2 oz (50g) Amaretti biscuits, broken into small pieces
4 oz (110g) plain flour
Pinch salt
2 oz (50g) butter, room temperature
2 oz (50g) caster sugar

For the topping
2 lbs (900g) Bramley cooking apples, peeled, cored and
   sliced
1 oz (25g) caster sugar
½ teaspoon cinnamon
1 oz (25g) melted butter

Preheat the oven to 180°C/Gas mark 4/Aga equivalent.

If you serve this for a dinner party, make it ahead of time to allow the base to set, as the hot apple juices transform the base into a marvellously chewy shortbread texture. Sift the flour and salt into a mixing bowl. Rub in the butter until the mixture resembles fine breadcrumbs (like making crumble), stir in the sugar and biscuit crumbs. Press this into a prepared 9 inch (23 cm) loose bottomed flan tin, lightly greased.

Either slice the apples by hand or use a processor to get thin, even slices. Arrange the apple slices by overlapping them to ensure that the base is completely covered and there are no gaps showing. Mix the sugar and cinnamon in a bowl. Brush the apples with melted butter and sprinkle over with the cinnamon sugar.

Bake in the oven on a high shelf for about 30-35 minutes or until the apples have softened and have caramelised around the edges. Leave the tart to cool in the tin before serving.

TREACLE TART

When I made the shoot lunch this was always a favourite – especially when everyone is cold and hungry.

Serves 8-10

For the pastry
10 oz (275g) plain flour
5 oz (150g) fat, butter and lard combined
Pinch of salt
This amount allows you to line the base of the tin and have enough left over to make a lattice pastry lid

For the filling
1½ lb (700g) golden syrup (1 tin)
Grated zest of 1 lemon
Approx 6 oz (175g) fresh breadcrumbs made from half a small loaf white bread

Preheat the oven to 200°C/Gas mark 6/Aga equivalent.

Make the pastry in the usual way and chill in the fridge for an hour.

Warm the syrup in a saucepan and add the lemon zest. Add the breadcrumbs and mix until all the syrup and breadcrumbs are well combined.

Line a 10 inch (25 cm) tin with about 8 oz (225g) of the pastry leaving the remainder for the top of the tart. Fill the pastry case with the syrup mixture. Roll out the remaining pastry and either use a lattice pastry cutter to cover the top or cut long strips of pastry and lay half vertically and half horizontally. Bake for about 30 minutes. Serve with hot custard or cream – or both.

TARTE AU CITRON

This has to be one of my all time favourite tarts. I like using a mix of lemon and lime juices for an even more citrussy flavour.

Serves 6

8 oz (225g) pâte sucrée

For the filling
5 fl oz (142ml carton) double cream
Juice and zest 3 limes and 2 lemons

4 eggs
6 oz (175g) caster sugar

Preheat the oven to 200°C/Gas mark 6/Aga equivalent.

Whisk the eggs and the sugar in a mixing bowl until thick and creamy. Stir in the cream and lemon and lime juices and mix well. Leave in the fridge until required.
When you're ready to cook the tart, roll out the pastry on a lightly floured board and line a 10 inch (25cm) metal flan tin. Prick the base and cook for about 20 minutes or until the pastry is golden.
Reduce the oven temperature to 150°C/Gas mark 2. Pour the lemon filling into the tart (the easiest method is to half pull out the cooked pastry case, pour the filling to the brim and slide back into the oven – you do need a steady hand to do this!). Bake the tart for a further 25-30 minutes. The filling should be slightly wobbly – it will continue to set once removed from the oven. Allow to cool. Serve with some crème fraîche or cream.

STRAWBERRY TART

This should look as professional as a tart from a French patisserie – it will certainly taste as good.

Serves 8

Approx 2 lb (1 kg) fresh strawberries

For the pastry:
8 oz (225g) pâte sucrée

Custard filling
If time is short, then I can highly recommend using a carton
    of quality supermarket custard. If time is not a problem,
    then make the home made variety:
½ pint (275ml) milk
3 egg yolks
2 oz (50g) sugar, flavoured with a vanilla pod
1 level tablespoon cornflour

For the glaze:
Juice 1 lemon
1 small pot of redcurrant jelly

Preheat the oven to 200°C/Gas mark 6/Aga equivalent.

Roll out the pâte sucrée pastry and line a 10 inch (25 cm) metal fluted tin. Bake for about 20 minutes or until lightly browned; remove from the oven and allow to cool.

To make the custard, heat the milk in a pan until hot. Place the egg yolks, sugar and cornflour in a bowl and whisk thoroughly together. Stir the hot milk into the egg and sugar mixture and whisk until smooth. Return this mixture to the pan, and stir over a gentle heat until the custard has thickened. Allow to cool, but stir every now and then to prevent a skin forming. Cover with cling film and chill in the fridge until required.

Spread the custard over the base of the tart. Cut the strawberries in half (or leave them whole if you prefer) and arrange in an attractive pattern over the custard. Melt the redcurrant jelly in a pan and add the lemon juice. Stir until the jelly has melted and is nice and runny. Spoon the glaze over the strawberries and serve when required.

Ready for Christmas

TARTE TATIN

Make this classic French tart using the best British apples!

Serves 4–6

4 oz (110g) butter
6 oz (170g) caster sugar
6-7 small Cox's Orange Pippin apples, peeled and cored
340g pack ready-made puff pastry

Preheat the oven to 200°C/Gas mark 6/Aga equivalent.

Choose the right pan for this recipe – ideally a heavy cast iron, oven-proof frying pan (no wooden or plastic handles or they will burn/melt in the oven). Ensure it is well scrubbed and was not previously used for frying garlic or anything else of a pungent and lingering nature!

Generously spread the butter evenly over the base and then sprinkle the sugar over the top. Peel the apples, then halve them and carefully remove the core. Press these down into the butter and sugar so that they fit nice and snugly, side by side, until the pan is full. Cook over a moderate heat until the butter and sugar caramelise and start to go a rich golden brown – this can take at least 20 minutes, but be patient. You will be rewarded with the most delicious taste if you are!

When the apples start going slightly brown round the edges and have fully absorbed all the butter and sugar, roll out the pastry so that it covers the top of the pan. Place over the apples and tuck in the edges so that you have, in effect, a pastry lid. Place the frying pan in the oven for about 20 minutes, or until the pastry has puffed up and is golden brown. Remove from the oven and stab the pastry in several places to allow the juices to soak through once you've turned it out. Now comes the tricky bit.

Get yourself an apron, some thick oven gloves and a large plate (bigger than the frying pan). Quickly turn the pan and plate over so you end up with the frying pan on top, face down. Carefully lift off the pan, and you should have some beautifully caramelised apples, drenched in an apple and caramel sauce sitting on top of light-as-a-feather pastry base. Serve with lashings of crème fraîche or vanilla ice cream.

CHAPTER 12

Well Preserved

In an ideal world I like to set aside a day for this. I enjoy picking fruit at our local P-Y-O, coming home for lunch and then getting down to the business of making the jam. For me, it is supremely satisfying, if a little smug-making, but seeing rows of home made jam in the larder really does cheer me up.

SEVILLE MARMALADE

I had made some pretty disastrous marmalade over the years until I was given this recipe – it works every time, without fail. Seville oranges only appear fleetingly in January, so make the most of their appearance.

3 lb (1.5kg) Seville oranges
2 large lemons
6 lb (3 kg) granulated sugar
4 pints (2 litres) water

Makes about 10 x 1 lb (450g) jars of marmalade.

Preheat the oven to 170°C/Gas mark 3/Aga equivalent.

Warm the sugar in the oven, as it will dissolve faster.

The easiest method I know is to soften the fruit first. Place the whole fruit in a large saucepan and cover with four pints of water. Put the lid on and bring to the boil; once it has come to the boil, remove and place the pan in the oven for about 2 hours, or until the fruit has softened. Once softened, remove the fruit from the pan (but keep the pan and water as you need it later) and place in a colander. Leave to cool for about half and hour. When cool enough to handle, cut each fruit in half and scoop out the flesh, pips and pith. Using a small, sharp serrated knife, really scrape out any remaining white pith so that all you're left with is the rind.

Place all this fruity flesh back into the pan with the water. Bring to the boil for about 6 minutes, and then strain this through a nylon sieve, really pressing the pulp through the sieve using a wooden spoon. The pulp contains all the pectin which is needed to make the marmalade set, so it's important to squeeze it through.

Cut up the orange rind as chunky or fine as you like. Place the pulpy liquid and rind in a preserving pan and add the sugar. Dissolve the sugar slowly until there are no remaining crystals. When completely dissolved, bring to the boil, and boil rapidly for about 10-15 minutes, or until set. Leave in the pan for about 20 minutes (this prevents the rind from floating to the top). Pour into warm, prepared jars. Seal and label.

Variations

If you like a dark marmalade, substitute 8 oz (225g) white sugar for 8 oz (225g) dark muscavado sugar instead.

For Whisky Marmalade, add approximately 8 tablespoons whisky to the marmalade once setting point has been reached.

THREE FRUIT MARMALADE

This is a very useful recipe to use when you're in the mood for making marmalade, but realise you've missed out on the Seville oranges. It's tangy and delicious.

3 grapefruit
2 large lemons
3 oranges (normal sweet ones)
6 pints (approx 3 litres) water
5 lb (2½ kg) granulated sugar

Make this in exactly the same way as Seville Marmalade. Cut the rind of the grapefruit, lemons and oranges into strips, either fine or chunky, depending on your preference.

Makes about 8 x 1 lb jars.

TOMATO RELISH

Just over 2 lb (1 kg) tomatoes, skins removed, and cut into small pieces
9 oz (250g) onions, finely chopped
2 cloves garlic, peeled and finely chopped
2 tablespoons salt
13 oz (375g) granulated sugar
2 teaspoons allspice
Approx ¾ pint (500ml) malt vinegar
1 tablespoon curry powder
2 teaspoons mustard powder
1 tablespoon cornflour

Place the tomatoes, onions and garlic in a large mixing bowl, and sprinkle over the salt. Stand for one hour. Then strain and discard the liquid. Place the mixture in a saucepan with the sugar, allspice and vinegar, and simmer gently for about 45 minutes, or until the tomatoes are soft and the mixture has reduced by half. Mix the curry powder, mustard and cornflour with a little vinegar to make a thin paste, add a few spoonfuls of the relish and return this to the pan. Cook for a further 5 minutes or until the relish has thickened. Pour the hot relish into prepared jars. Seal when cold. This will keep for up to one year.

RASPBERRY JAM

This is pretty much fool proof, and easier than making strawberry jam which I have to confess doesn't always work. This does, year in, year out.

4 lb (1¾ kg) raspberries, hulled
4 lb (1¾ kg) granulated sugar

Put some saucers in the freezer for testing later. Make sure your jam jars have been washed in hot water, dried and placed in a moderate oven (180°C/Gas mark 4/Aga equivalent) for a minimum of 5 minutes. Add the jam while they are still hot. You will need about 6 x 1 lb jars with lids (unless you prefer using paper covers).

Place the sugar in a preserving pan, add the raspberries and gently heat through until the sugar has dissolved, stirring from time to time. You must make sure that every bit of sugar has properly dissolved – it does take about 20 minutes. By now you will have a lovely thick syrupy mix and you can turn up the heat. You need to get it to boil rapidly until the setting point has been achieved. Start testing after 3-4 minutes of rapid boiling. Put a teaspoon of jam on the ice-cold saucer, allow to cool slightly. Gently push your finger through the jam to see if it wrinkles – if it does, it has reached setting point. Turn off the heat, take the jam jars out of the oven and place on baking trays (you are bound to spill some and it makes washing up easier).

Give the jam a good stir before pouring into the jars. I find it easier to decant some jam into a large jug and then pour into the jars, filling up to the top. I don't bother with fiddly paper covers; I just screw on the lids and label, fill up the shelves and bask in glory.

132

Jam making is hot work

CHAPTER 13

Fancy Liquors

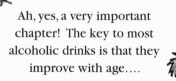

Ah, yes, a very important chapter! The key to most alcoholic drinks is that they improve with age....

SLOE GIN...OR VODKA

1 lb (450g) sloes
1 bottle gin or vodka
1 lb (450g) granulated white sugar
2-3 drops of almond essence

Give the sloes a quick rinse and place in a plastic container (an empty ice-cream tub is perfect). Put them in the freezer – this will cause them to burst which means there is no need to prick each sloe (a rather tedious task).

When you're ready to make the gin/vodka, take the sloes out of the freezer and allow to defrost thoroughly. Using a funnel, decant the sloes into a large 1 litre screw top bottle (which has been sterilised first). Pour in the sugar and top up to the neck with gin or vodka (it takes almost all of a 75 cl bottle) – this needs a steady hand. Add 2-3 drops almond essence, screw the top on firmly and give it a good shake. Place in a warm, dark place like an airing cupboard and leave for as long as possible. When you can remember, give the bottle a good shake every now and then for the first couple of weeks. Allow to mature!

When you can't wait any longer, take a sterilised empty bottle and place a funnel over the hole (ideally lined with a coffee filter paper, or a muslin cloth). Strain the liquid into the bottle, screw on the top and drink when your morale needs lifting. Keep the left-over sloes for a delicious chocolate recipe at the end of the chapter. Sloe gin/vodka are perfect for the following:

SLOE GIN AND TONIC

Pour an inch of sloe gin into a tall glass, top with cold tonic and fill with ice – this makes a very refreshing summer drink.

SLOEGASM

Pour ½ inch of sloe gin into a champagne glass and top up with champagne.

BLOODY MARY

This is the business on a Sunday morning while you read the papers and let some slave cook lunch!

Vodka
Dry sherry
A dash of Tabasco
Tablespoon Worcestershire
    sauce
Freshly ground black pepper
¼ teaspoon paprika
Juice of 1-2 lemons
Pinch of celery salt
Teaspoon horseradish sauce
1 bottle fresh chilled tomato
    juice – use a good quality.
    brand

Pour an inch of vodka and ½ inch of dry sherry into a large glass jug. Pour in the chilled tomato juice and fill to a sensible height. Season well with the ingredients listed – use your judgement on how spicy you like to flavour the juice. Add the lemon juice and mix thoroughly. You could also add a few sticks of celery to the jug for just a bit more flavour.

ELDERFLOWER CORDIAL

The most refreshing cordial ever, and really easy to make.

25 heads elderflower in full flower
4 oranges
1 lemon
3 lb (1½ kg) granulated sugar
2 oz (60g) tartaric or citric acid
3 pints water

Gently dissolve the sugar in the water in a large preserving pan. Take off the heat and add the elderflower heads. Squeeze the juice from the oranges and lemons into the water; roughly chop the skins and add to the water. Add the tartaric acid and stir thoroughly. Cover with a clean teatowel and leave for 48 hours.
Strain through a sieve lined with a muslin cloth and pour into clean glass bottles.

Dilute to drink.

LEMON VODKA

Bottle of vodka
3 unwaxed lemons, peeled and cut into strips

Remove the top 2 inches (5cm) of liquid from a full bottle of (you may just have to drink this!). Remove the peel from the lemons, slice in strips, and push down into the neck of the bottle. Screw the top back on and give it a good shake. Leave in a cupboard for several months.

The vodka is ready to drink when it is golden yellow in colour. Put the bottle in the freezer and serve either as shots or 'on the rocks' over ice.

RASPBERRY GIN

This would make a wonderful Christmas present.

Bottle of gin
1 lb (450g) fresh raspberries (approximately)
White sugar

Find a clean, empty wide-necked mineral water bottle. Fill to the shoulder with raspberries, leaving a 2 inch (5cm) gap to the top. Fill to the brim with sugar, and pour in the gin using a funnel. As the gin goes in it dissolves the sugar, but leave about an inch of space at the top. Screw on the lid and shake whenever you can remember to. Leave for as long as possible (at least three months, preferably until Christmas!).

Elderflower wine is most refreshing

CHAPTER 14

Nibbles

I am addicted to nibbles, be they crisps, dips, whatever. I've included a
few family favourites.

CHEESE STRAWS

These are delicious. Serve as a pre-lunch or dinner snack with a glass of wine…or two!

6 oz (175g) of mature Cheddar cheese, grated
8 oz (225g) self-raising flour
4 oz (110g) butter
1 egg yolk
Pinch of salt
1 teaspoon baking powder
½ teaspoon cayenne pepper, or paprika if you prefer
½ teaspoon chilli powder (if you like a slightly hotter taste, make it 1 teaspoon each of cayenne and chilli)

Preheat the oven to 200°C/Gas mark 6/Aga equivalent.

Sift together the flour, baking powder, salt, cayenne pepper and chilli powder. Rub in the butter. Add the egg yolk.

Knead in the grated cheese until you have formed a dough-shaped ball. Roll out onto a lightly floured surface and cut into finger length strips. Place the strips onto a lightly greased baking tray and bake for approx. 10 minutes or until light golden brown and crisp. Remove from the oven and allow to cool on a wire rack before serving.

SAUSAGES IN HONEY AND SESAME SEEDS

40 cocktail sausages (or 20 chipolatas, cut in half)
Approx. 4 tablespoons clear honey
Approx. 2 tablespoons sesame seeds

Lay the sausages out on a baking tray. Drizzle about 4 tablespoons clear honey over the sausages and sprinkle with sesame seeds. Bake in hot oven for about 15-20 minutes. Spike each sausage with a cocktail stick and serve hot.

QUAILS' EGGS AND MAYONNAISE

Hard boil the eggs and peel the shells (a slightly fiddly job, I'm afraid). Serve on a platter with a bowl of mayonnaise and/or a dish of freshly ground black pepper and salt mixed together, or celery salt.

DEVILS ON HORSEBACK

10 rashers streaky bacon
20 no-soak prunes

Cut the rashers in half. Place a prune on a slice of bacon and roll up. Bake in a hot oven for about 15 minutes.

CROSTINI

1 stick French bread
1 garlic clove, peeled and halved
1 jar roasted red pepper paste
Olive oil

Cut the bread into ½ inch (1 cm) diagonal slices and rub with the garlic clove. Drizzle with olive oil and bake in a hot oven for about 5-10 minutes, or until golden. Remove from the oven and spread with the red pepper paste.

DOLCELATTE DIP

Arrange a selection of crudités (carrot batons, strips of red pepper, cucumber, celery etc) on a large platter with the dip sitting in the middle.

5 fl oz (150ml) sour cream or crème fraîche
1 garlic clove, peeled and crushed
6 oz (175g) Dolcelatte
Juice 1 lemon
Salt and pepper
Tablespoon chopped chives, to garnish

Place all the ingredients in a food processor and whizz until smooth. Adjust the seasoning and garnish with chopped chives.

BOURSIN DIP

1 tub (200g) Philadelphia cream cheese
1 x 80g pack of Boursin
Drop of milk (optional)

Mix the two cheeses together, adding a drop of milk if necessary. Simplicity itself!

WINE TASTING

Examination

Rotation

Anticipation

Appreciation

AUBERGINE DIP

2 small aubergines
4 cloves garlic, peeled and sliced
Salt and pepper
1 teaspoon soy sauce
4 tablespoons olive oil
1 tomato, chopped (skinned and de-seeded)
2 oz (50g) toasted pine nuts

Preheat the oven to 180°C/Gas mark 4/Aga equivalent

Cut the aubergines in half and make slits all over for the garlic slivers. Sprinkle with salt, place on a baking tray and cook for an hour in a moderate oven. Remove from oven and allow to cool. Scoop out the flesh into the bowl of a food processor, and add the remaining ingredients and pulse till smooth. Check the seasoning. Refrigerate until required. Serve with triangles of hot pitta bread.

MINI PIZZAS

Preheat the oven to 180°C/Gas mark 4/Aga equivalent.

Cheat, and buy your favourite type of pizza. Use your smallest pastry cutter to cut out circles; lay on a baking tray and cook in a moderate oven for about 10 minutes, or until bubbling.

SLOE CHOCOLATES

When you've finished making the gin, use the de-stoned, left-over sloes to make these delicious chocolates.

Place the sloes on a baking tray lined with greaseproof paper. Meanwhile, melt a large bar of quality dark chocolate in a bowl over gently simmering water. Pour the melted chocolate over the sloes and allow to cool. When completely cold, cut up into squares and serve with coffee for the ultimate after dinner chocolates.

CONVERSION TABLES

Use imperial or metric, but whatever you do, don't mix them together!

The conversions used are based on these weights:

		Volume	
½ oz	10g		
½ oz	20g	2 fl oz	55ml
1 oz	25g	3 fl oz	75ml
1½ oz	40g	5 fl oz (¼ pint)	150ml
2 oz	50g	10 fl oz (½ pint)	275ml
2½ oz	60g	1 pint	570ml
3 oz	75g	1¼ pints	725ml
4 oz	110g	1¾ pints	1 litre
4½ oz	125g	2 pints	1.2 litres
5 oz	150g	2½ pints	1.5 litres
6 oz	175g	4 pints	2.25 litres
7 oz	200g		
8 oz	225g		
9 oz	250g		
10 oz	275g		
12 oz	350g		
1 lb	450g		
1 lb 8 oz	700g		
2 lb	900g		
3 lb	1.35 kilos		

OVEN TEMPERATURES

I have to be honest and say that not every recipe has been tested on every type of oven. I acquired a 2 door Aga a year ago, but up until then I cooked on gas and electric cookers. I am sure that anyone reading this book will know whether their own oven is slightly hotter, or cooler than the timings suggest, and will use their common sense accordingly.

Oven temperatures

Gas mark 1	275°F	140°C
Gas mark 2	300	150
Gas mark 3	325	170
Gas mark 4	350	180
Gas mark 5	375	190
Gas mark 6	400	200
Gas mark 7	425	220
Gas mark 8	450	230
Gas mark 9	475	240

LIST OF RECIPES